Reflective Teaching and Learning in Further Education

**FURTHER
EDUCATION**

You might also like the following FE books from Critical Publishing

A Complete Guide to the Level 4 Certificate in Education and Training
Lynn Machin, Duncan Hindmarch, Sandra Murray and Tina Richardson
978-1-909330-89-4

A Complete Guide to the Level 5 Diploma in Education and Training
Lynn Machin, Duncan Hindmarch, Sandra Murray and Tina Richardson
978-1-909682-53-5

The A-Z Guide to Working in Further Education
Jonathan Gravells and Susan Wallace
978-1-909330-85-6

Equality and Diversity in Further Education
Sheine Peart 978-1-909330-97-9

Inclusion in Further Education
Lydia Spenceley 978-1-909682-05-4

The Professional Teacher in Further Education
Keith Appleyard and Nancy Appleyard 978-1-909682-01-6

Teaching and Supporting Adult Learners
Jackie Scruton and Belinda Ferguson 978-1-909682-13-9

Teaching in Further Education: The Inside Story
Sue Wallace 978-1-909682-73-3

Understanding the Further Education Sector: A Critical Guide to Policies and Practices
Susan Wallace 978-1-909330-21-4

Most of our titles are also available in a range of electronic formats. To order please go to our website www.criticalpublishing.com or contact our distributor, NBN International, 10 Thornbury Road, Plymouth PL6 7PP, telephone 01752 202301 or email orders@nbninternational.com.

Reflective Teaching and Learning in Further Education

 Nancy and Keith Appleyard

Series Editor Susan Wallace

FURTHER
EDUCATION

First published in 2015 by Critical Publishing Ltd

British Library Cataloguing in Publication Data
A CIP record for this book is available from the British Library

ISBN: 978-1-909682-85-6

This book is also available in the following e-book formats:

MOBI ISBN: 978-1-909682-86-3
EPUB ISBN: 978-1-909682-87-0
Adobe e-book: 978-1-909682-88-7

Cover and text design by Greensplash Limited
Project Management by Out of House Publishing
Printed and bound in Great Britain by Bell & Bain, Glasgow

Critical Publishing
152 Chester Road
Northwich
CW8 4AL
www.criticalpublishing.com

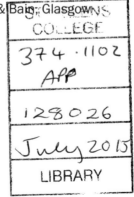

Contents

Meet the authors

Nancy Appleyard

I am a social anthropologist with a specialism in language, communication and human interaction. My early working life was in the insurance industry, initially with a large general insurance company and then as a partner in a commercial insurance brokerage. A career change brought me to Lincoln College where I taught insurance, business skills and communication studies. My particular interest is supporting learners in developing their professional and personal relationships through effective communication.

Keith Appleyard

I have worked in further education (FE) since 1978 as a teacher, college senior manager and teacher trainer. I have been a tutor and course leader for PGCE/Cert Ed programmes at Lincoln College, and a tutor and franchise co-ordinator on these programmes at Nottingham Trent University. Most recently I have worked as an initial teacher training reviewer for Standards Verification UK and as a consultant for LSIS. I live in Lincolnshire and, with my wife Nancy, am the co-author of three other books on FE issues.

Meet the series editor

Susan Wallace

I am Emeritus Professor of Education at Nottingham Trent University where, for many years, part of my role was to support learning on the initial training courses for teachers in the further education (FE) sector. I taught in the sector myself for ten years, including on BTEC programmes and basic skills provision. My particular interest is in the motivation and behaviour of students in FE, and in mentoring and the ways in which a successful mentoring relationship can support personal and professional development. I have written a range of books, mainly aimed at teachers and student teachers in the sector, and I enjoy hearing readers' own stories of FE, whether it is by email or at speaking engagements and conferences.

Acknowledgements

Our grateful thanks to:

Vicki Locke and all her colleagues in the Teaching and Learning Hub at Boston College for showing us how the 'Journey to Outstanding' (J2O) project operates and welcoming our participation;

Lydia Spenceley at Grantham College, Jo Campbell at Boston College and all the ITT trainees who talked to us about their own experiences and gave us such useful feedback;

Susan Wallace and Julia Morris for their advice and continuing support.

1 Introduction

The old grey donkey, Eeyore, stood by himself in a thistly corner of the Forest, his front feet well apart, his head on one side, and thought about things. Sometimes he thought ... to himself, 'Why?' and sometimes he thought, 'Wherefore?' and sometimes he thought, 'Inasmuch as which?'

Milne, 2000, p 74

Everybody reflects, even fictitious donkeys! And this particular donkey has enlisted the help of some rather useful reflective words: *'Why?'*, *'Wherefore?'* and *'Inasmuch as which?'* If Eeyore were really to push the reflective boat out perhaps he could come up with some more handy words; words such as *'What?'*, *'If?'*, *'How?'*, *'What else?'* and *'Supposing?'* to name just a few.

Of course, for Eeyore in his thistly corner of the forest, the concept of reflective practice is no more real than Eeyore himself, so he probably does not need to bother. But the same cannot be said for anyone teaching in further education (FE). Indeed, in FE it is difficult to avoid hearing about, reading about or participating in discussion on reflective practice. Scholarly articles on the subject abound; educational libraries have dozens of books on the topic and teacher training courses invariably have reflective practice as a key element of their course design. This is no coincidence, nor is it overkill.

Why reflective practice is so important

There are three main reasons why reflective practice has become so significant: firstly the influence of educational theorists, secondly the concept of the teacher as an autonomous professional and finally the introduction of government regulation designed to ensure high standards of teaching in the FE sector.

The influence of educational theorists

During the second half of the last century, educational theory witnessed a change in emphasis away from concentrating on didactic skills where the teacher's job was to impart knowledge and skills to a passive audience. Rather the teacher was increasingly seen as a facilitator of learning, and the focus was centred on the learners rather than the teacher.

One of the most influential writers in this regard was David Kolb. His 1983 book *Experiential Learning* proposed a model involving reflective practice as a key teaching skill whereby the teacher reflects on and analyses a teaching problem prior to identifying ways of solving it and trying out possible alternative strategies. Around the same time, Donald Schön proposed that reflective practice was an indispensible characteristic of effective teaching, and that teachers gradually build up the ability to reflect in an increasingly sophisticated manner throughout their careers. Other writers have developed these theories – Graham Gibbs, Gary Rolph and Chris Johns, for example – and in consequence, developing the skills of critical reflection has now become an indispensible element of the training and professional development of FE teachers.

The teacher as an autonomous professional

This trend to incorporate reflective practice in the skill set of FE teachers has been partly driven by the perception of FE teachers as autonomous professionals: well-trained teachers delivering a high quality product and with considerable discretion on how they carried out their work in the classroom. Consequently, the vast majority of initial teacher training (ITT) courses in the late twentieth century included a strong focus on reflective practice with novice FE teachers being required to reflect on the lessons they taught, to keep a learning journal and to discuss their successes, problems and feelings with colleagues, mentors and tutors.

In this context, reflective practice was seen as an emancipatory and individualised experience that was encouraged and supported on a voluntary basis by most college managements. For FE teachers the emphasis was on intrinsic rewards; enthusiasm for reflective practice was a good attitude to develop because it would improve your teaching and increase your personal satisfaction in doing a rewarding professional job.

Government regulation

Increasing government regulation is the third reason why reflective practice has become so ubiquitous within the FE sector. At the time that writers like Kolb and Schön were encouraging teachers to become reflective practitioners, successive governments started to adopt policies that were designed to make the teaching profession more efficient and accountable.

Before 2001, there was no mandatory requirement for teachers in FE to hold a recognised teaching qualification. The tradition in the sector was that the key requirement for vocational teachers was experience and qualifications in their subject specialism. If you wanted somebody to teach welding, your prime need would be to find an expert welder; their teaching skills could be acquired on the job or by undertaking a part-time teaching course. A significant number of teachers did undertake part-time qualifications such as City and Guilds 7407, PGCE or Cert Ed and were supported by their employers in doing this. However, as gaining an ITT qualification was not mandatory, there were many teachers in the sector with no teaching qualification and little involvement with the ideas of reflective practice.

This rather ad hoc and haphazard system came under the political spotlight, particularly following the 1997 election and Tony Blair's mantra of his priorities as *'Education, education, education!'*. In 1998 it became government policy that all teachers in FE should not only be teacher trained but also that this training should meet agreed national standards. The aim of this policy was to raise the status of the teaching profession to equate with that of other professional occupational areas such as medicine or law. Service users and other stakeholders needed a guarantee that learners in FE would be taught by well-trained teachers working to high professional standards.

The result of this policy has been the design of a succession of written standards that are intended to guarantee a professional service delivered by well-trained and motivated teachers. The first set of standards, known as the Further Education National Training Organisation (FENTO) standards, was published in 2001. These were superseded in 2007 by the Lifelong Learning UK (LLUK) standards. There was an additional mandatory requirement that FE teachers would need a qualification that met these standards in order to gain a licence to practice. Since the publication of the Lingfield report in 2011, this policy has been modified to encompass a less centralised approach. At the time of writing, the FE sector is working with the 2014 Education and Training Foundation (ETF) set of professional standards, which, like its predecessors, has a strong focus on reflective practice.

In summary, reflective practice is here to stay, a key professional skill for FE teachers, supported by current educational theory and encouraged by government regulation. This is why it is so important and worth investigation.

About this book

This book is an examination of reflective practice, primarily intended for all teachers working in FE, no matter which part of the sector you are working in and what stage of your career you have reached. A basic premise is that reflective practice is a skill not only for the professional role of the FE teacher, but it is also a life skill providing a philosophical basis for a wise and fulfilling life.

Content

The content of the book is designed to help you become a more effective reflective practitioner. It moves from an introduction to reflective practice to a consideration of a series of key themes relevant to the work of an FE teacher within which effective reflective practice is illustrated. The final part of the book aims to encourage a deeper understanding of reflective practice by offering a critique of the concept in the light of the issues introduced earlier. There is consequently a progression from the earlier chapters, where the emphasis is on practical situations, to the final chapters, where there is a greater focus on the philosophical basis of reflective practice.

Here it is worth commenting on the use of educational theory. Your understanding of reflective practice will be formed from a variety of sources: your personal teaching experience, discussions with colleagues, reading, formal training courses, casual chats with friends and so on. The content of this book reflects this variety, using case studies and the authors' personal experiences to illustrate the main learning points, alongside material drawn from a range of writers and theorists whose insights have contributed to the understanding of reflective practice. Hence, educational theory has an important contribution to the narrative of this book, increasingly so as ideas are developed in greater depth in the later chapters. However, the emphasis is always on the practical experience of teachers as the starting point for understanding reflective practice, while theory is seen as supporting and enriching this experience.

Chapter content

Chapter 2 introduces the concept of reflective practice through the eyes of professional practitioners. It covers its processes and key features, emphasising the need to match these to your own individual requirements.

Chapters 3–6 look at reflective practice in action, starting with the theme of planning and the practicalities of teaching. Chapter 3 focuses on developing and maintaining these skills and, as in all other sections of the book, uses case studies and appropriate theory to illustrate how the chapter theme can be integrated within your reflective practice. The theme of Chapter 4 is the relationship between reflective practice and self-awareness, considering issues relating to personality, personal strengths, beliefs and values. Chapter 5 is concerned with communicating and managing behaviour, and uses examples from a range of teaching and learning situations to demonstrate the importance and value of critical reflection in developing effective communication techniques and behaviour management skills. Chapter 6 highlights reflective practice as a cornerstone of continuing professional development (CPD). Through a series of case studies you will be encouraged to engage in reflective practice in order to identify, plan, undertake and evaluate your own developmental activities.

The final three substantive chapters develop the themes introduced earlier. Chapter 7 is a more in-depth study of reflective practice. It traces its development and its increasing popularity since the work of Dewey in the 1930s and reviews recent theory in the context of contemporary FE teaching. It describes how reflective practice has been used in a variety of professions as a tool for professional development and is now an important element of government encouragement for FE teachers to attain and develop high standards of professionalism.

Chapter 8 evaluates the potential limitations of reflective practice and balances these against its benefits. This chapter emphasises the need to be realistic about what it can achieve but suggests that, even in an unsympathetic environment, there are many ways in which reflective practice enriches professional life.

Chapter 9 introduces action research as a key method of developing reflective practice further, leading to a deeper understanding of its power and range. It highlights the philosophy of action research, looks at its key features and uses an in-depth case study to illustrate the role of reflection in action research. The aim is to inspire you to engage in your own action research as a means of developing your skills as a reflective practitioner. This point is reinforced in the conclusion (Chapter 10).

Structure and use

Each chapter, apart from this introduction and the conclusion, follows the same structure that includes:

- a statement of aims that outlines the purpose and rationale for the chapter, plus a visual map that depicts the chapter content;

- an introduction that briefly outlines the chapter content;

- case studies that give practical examples of the learning points under consideration, together with questions for discussion and further research;

- critical thinking activities designed to draw out the relevance of the chapter content to your own reflective practice;

- a conclusion and chapter reflections that summarise the content and learning points of the chapter;

- suggestions for further reading headed 'Taking it further';

- references.

There are many terms in common use to describe teachers and learners: lecturer, trainer, tutor, instructor, student and client come to mind. Normally this depends on where you are working, but for the purposes of this book the generic terms *teacher* and *learner* are used throughout the narrative.

The case studies that you will find throughout the book are based on real-life situations. In these studies you are asked to consider certain points, and hopefully to relate the situation to your own experience. They are designed to stimulate thought and discussion.

The critical thinking activities are designed to help you consolidate and develop what you have learned. They encourage you to think about a particular aspect of the chapter and relate it to your own practice and to the theoretical concepts discussed in the chapter. They also give you the opportunity to explore these concepts in relation to your own situation.

These features should help you to develop as a reflective practitioner no matter what your professional role is and how much you already know about reflective practice. You will want and need different things from your reading dependent on your professional situation and experience. If the whole concept is new to you, the book may well serve as a practical introduction that can be related to meeting the everyday challenges facing you in your work. Alternatively, if you are interested in the philosophical aspects of reflective practice you may find the later sections covering theory and research most useful. The main premise is that anyone working in the FE sector – novice teachers, teacher training tutors, experienced teachers – will be able to enhance their skills as reflective practitioners.

2 What is reflective practice?

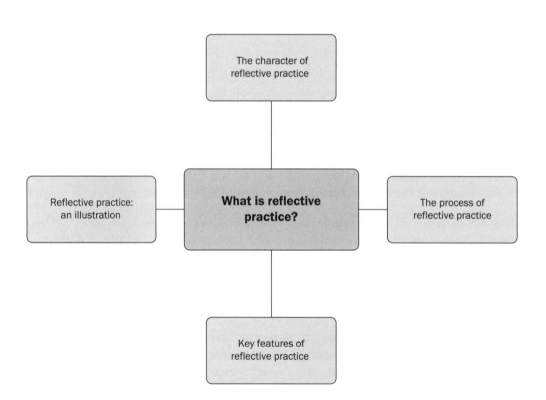

Chapter aims

This chapter will help you to:

- understand the character of reflective practice;

- understand the process of reflective practice;

- identify the key features of reflective writing and practice;

- identify the main characteristics of your own reflective practice.

Introduction

Trying to pin down reflective practice, putting your finger on what it involves, is not easy. Moreover, it is likely to mean something different to each of us. You could even say it is as individual as you are. Now this is not very helpful if you are looking to develop your professional practice – it is even worse if you are just beginning as a teacher and trying to figure it out. Yet, while it would make no sense to apply a reflective practice label indiscriminately, there is much to be gained from taking some of its basic building blocks and constructing them in a way that works for you. And really, this is how it needs to be. If reflective practice is to have any meaning and value for you as an individual, it has to be your own bespoke version.

This chapter is an introduction to some of those building blocks or key themes that will be developed in subsequent chapters. It opens with a brief review of reflective practice in the wider context. It continues with teachers talking about how they feel about it and how they find their own ways to reflect. The chapter then explores the process of reflective practice and identifies a number of its key features.

The character of reflective practice

Who reflects?

If asked whether they reflect, many people would struggle to work out what exactly was meant by the question. This should not be too surprising because reflection is not a subject that is generally discussed. Yet it is odd why this should be the case as reflecting is an activity that we all engage in even though it is one we seldom talk about. Reflection is certainly alive and kicking in the public sphere. Sports people and commentators are good examples with public agonies over missed opportunities, '*How on earth did I manage to miss that shot?*' or '*If only we'd passed the ball when we had the chance!*'

It seems we have been reflecting for a long time. Since way back when we first became fully human we have possessed the ability to look back and then to use what we have learnt to plan forward. Mary Warnock suggests that

> *... humans alone have developed an awareness of their own position in the world, and an ability to think of the past and future, as well as the present, the absent*

as well as what is in front of their eyes, what they would like to be as well as what they are.

(Warnock, 1998, pp 107–8)

If you take a look at some of the ancient philosophies you will discover that reflection occupies a central and valuable place. The Roman Emperor Marcus Aurelius and the Greek philosopher Epictetus were skilled reflectors and Socrates is known for urging people to examine their lives. Similar ideas appear in Hinduism, Taoism, Confucianism and Buddhism where self-reflection is viewed as a step towards attaining wisdom. Confucius for example said, '*Whoever knows essentially his own nature, can know also that of other men*'. These philosophers were not talking about idle musings or the venting of frustrations at missing a goal but about structured, logical self-examination.

Because these philosophers were writing centuries ago, you could be forgiven for thinking that their ideas have limited relevance nowadays and that perhaps this type of structured reflection is only to be found in teaching and training. But this is not the case. Reflective practice is very much alive and kicking right across the professional board. Here are some professionals talking about their own experience of reflecting.

- Ann-Marie Kerr, designer: *Self-reflection is an automatic response for me. I have been doing it since I was an art student and it has become a habit.*

- Manjula Kurni, consultant gynaecologist: *Yes, I do it every day, almost automatically in my daily practice and with my family. I think it is very important to reflect and improve your practice and your skills.*

- Wade Rowlett, construction consultant: *I think I reflect naturally. To me it's about improving everything you do.*

- Edward Gayton, dental surgeon: *I look back at my day and ask myself what went well and what didn't go quite as well and why. I think this is something any professional will do.*

How do you reflect?

Reflective practice occupies a somewhat dubious and precarious position in the popularity stakes for many teachers. This can be illustrated by the comments of a number of teachers who are working towards the Diploma in Education and Training. Here they are talking about how they feel about reflective practice.

CASE STUDIES

Jessica, occupational therapist teaching art

It's an important part of teaching – but also life in general. The reflecting part is OK – it's putting that into practice and actioning what you have reflected on that's difficult.

Kayleigh, teaching employment skills

At first I found it difficult but it became much easier after I had been teaching a while. It is an important part of development but it is not always easy to identify areas for improvement and what to do about it.

Michael, RAF technician teaching radar

I think sometimes reflection helps us on the journey to aim higher but can also pull us down if not in the correct frame of mind.

Jorge, teaching sports studies

I think reflection is useful but realistically I do not get the time to reflect on every lesson. Due to my heavy workload it often seems like a waste of time.

Scott, teaching motor vehicle technology

I reflect continually (mentally) but don't always find the time to write/record my reflections, which I feel lets me down.

Suzanne, police service teaching support for vulnerable adults

I think reflective practice is key to improvement. However, I feel you need a certain level of confidence to be able to constructively reflect. I don't like reflective practice as I'm not confident and take everything to heart.

Jakub, construction lecturer teaching brickwork

It's sometimes good but personally I tend to be ultra critical, so reflective practice could be initially bad but overall useful.

From these comments it seems that while the value of reflective practice is not in doubt, actually doing it is another thing altogether, and it is not difficult to work out the reasons why.

The most glaring culprit in this scenario is finding the time to actually fit reflection in to what is often a very busy and demanding schedule. But it is not just a matter of time. For many it is not easy to get a handle on what is involved. On the one hand it should be simple; if it is natural, something we all do then it should be easy to do. Yet, it seems frighteningly complex.

A further problem is that reflecting connects with the essence of who you are and requires honest self-examination. This can seem daunting, challenging and even risky; you could be in for a rough ride. Reflective practice implies being self-critical, accepting that you have made mistakes and need to do things better in future. This does not do much for your confidence levels, especially if you are also starting to come to terms with a complex new skill. So a certain reluctance to engage with reflective practice is certainly understandable.

Critical thinking activity

»   *How would you describe your own attitude and feelings about using reflective practice in your professional life?*

Doubtless you have some sympathy with the difficulties expressed by the teachers in the case studies above. However, despite their reservations there is the sense that they consider reflecting to be a worthwhile activity. The question now is, how do you reconcile this difference; in other words, how do you engage in an activity which you know is worthwhile but which you also know is not necessarily going to be easy or problem free?

Getting started

Although at first glance it may appear counter-intuitive, probably the best mindset you can have for reflective practice is to approach it with gusto, grabbing hold with both hands and hanging on, taking control of your own reflective practice and making it work for you. The twentieth-century philosopher and educationalist John Dewey (1933) must have had something of this in mind when he spoke of *'wholeheartedness'* as an essential attribute of reflective practice.

This approach involves making a commitment to yourself to *study* yourself. One way to do this is to imagine yourself as a project that you are going to research; an exploration of what you do and why you do it. It also means looking at the values, assumptions and emotions that inform your actions, but as a detached researcher it becomes a bit easier. One reward you get from taking this approach is the ownership you feel of your reflective practice – you are the expert with regard to yourself after all. As Peter Tarrant points out:

> *... it should be the person doing the reflecting who gets the most out of the experience. In order to manage this, they should have some ownership of the process, they should see and understand its purpose and should not feel that it is something imposed upon them by others.*
>
> (Tarrant, 2013, p 2)

Taking ownership means the experience itself becomes more rewarding because you are doing it your way. A further spin-off concerns the insights you gain about yourself, insights about you as a person acting and interacting with others around you, not only with regard to your professional teaching but with your colleagues, family members, friends and so on.

As for the practicalities of how you set about your reflective practice, a good starting point is to look at how you might initiate the action of reflecting. As a teacher it is likely, although not necessarily the case, that it will be triggered by an experience from your teaching which you will want to take time to consider. In an ideal professional world there would be no frustrations and no time constraints. But you know that is not going to happen. Nevertheless, the opportunity to reflect needs to be incorporated somewhere – but where and how?

Opportunities to reflect

It is worth returning to those seven teachers who voiced their feelings about their own experience of reflecting. They are talking here about how they manage to reflect as part of their busy lives.

CASE STUDIES

Jessica

As part of my organisation's CPD programme I regularly attend an informal group where we share thoughts over a coffee. Pooling problems and ideas get us all thinking and we all gain.

Kayleigh

Reflecting is pretty much ongoing, part of my life. I don't know whether I am a natural reflector or have just been doing it in my teaching for so many years but it's second nature for me to reflect on what I am experiencing or have experienced. I do it automatically and more or less unconsciously.

Michael

I incorporated an extra column in my session plans to remind me to think about each session and jot down some notes to myself while it is still fresh in my mind. Then I set aside a regular time to go over my jottings – I make a point of going over in my mind how a session went. Learning to reflect is a big part of the course and we are encouraged to get into the habit of doing it regularly.

Jorge

Once I finish teaching for the day I capture my thoughts on my mobile while it's still in my mind and sort it out later. On the occasions I've not managed to do this I've found I've lost most of it.

Scott

What's working for me at the moment is to make a point of going over how a session went the first chance I get after we have finished – not easy as we are pretty rushed at the moment but I usually manage to find a quiet minute or two at some point. And I'm one of those people who has the best insights when they are most relaxed. In fact I can often have quite a productive conversation with myself last thing at night.

Suzanne

I think it's helpful to have someone to talk to and use as a sounding board. I think a colleague is good as they are likely to have had similar experiences and often say something that can get me thinking. I also have a supportive mentor who has been sitting in on one or two of my classes and he has provided useful feedback and given me a lot to think about.

Jakub

I try to make a point of asking my learners to give me some feedback on a session; what was useful or not, what they found difficult, enjoyable and so on. It usually gives me useful ideas to explore.

Critical thinking activity

Think about your own experiences of reflecting.

» *How do you set about it?*

» *Which of the above examples do you identify with and why?*

» *Are there any other opportunities to reflect that you could explore?*

You are likely to have noticed from these examples that people have different ways of setting about reflecting and that there is no one right way; it takes place in different ways depending on who you are, on the situation and on the stage you have reached in your professional life. What is important is for you to find your own ways for reflecting, of trying out various options to see what works for you and to take advantage of any opportunities that present themselves. The goal with each of these methods is the same: reflection becomes automatic, intuitive and ongoing.

You may also have noticed from the examples that *sooner, little and often* seems to work for these teachers, a better approach than *later and bitten off in big chunks*. This should not surprise anyone who has tried to get fit – for most of us, a 20-minute walk taken now, or a short sharp stint on the exercise bike is easier to manage than looking ahead to spending hours at the gym.

Ways of reflecting

Having identified how you might set about reflecting, the next point to consider is what happens when you reflect. What are you engaged in doing when you reflect? Obviously, it is going to be something more than idle thoughts running through your mind, although, oddly, the act of emptying your mind of the hundred and one things you need to be doing can be immensely helpful. The Greek philosopher Pythagoras (580–500 BCE), who sought to interpret the entire physical world in terms of numbers and whose famous theorem you will remember from your school days, offers the following advice. '*Learn to be silent. Let your quiet mind listen and absorb*'.

Emptying your mind of the humdrum allows space for more productive ideas to enter. As to how this works in practice, you are likely to have identified from the above examples that reflecting involves initiating a conversation or dialogue. This might be a self-dialogue, a conversation you have with yourself. Michael and Scott's comments are good examples of self-dialogue: '*I make a point of going over in my mind how a session went*' and '*I have quite a productive conversation with myself*'.

The dialogue can also be one that involves others. This might be a single other, as illustrated by Suzanne's comments: '*I think a colleague is good as they are likely to have had similar experiences and often say something that can get me thinking*'. It can also be a group dialogue as in Jessica's case: '*I regularly attend an informal group where we share thoughts over a coffee*'. Ghaye and Ghaye (1998) highlight the importance of both forms of dialogue, suggesting that reflective dialogue may begin as a self-conversation but it should then move into the public sphere. By far the greater proportion of this dialogue will be in the form of the conversations you have with yourself as you reflect on your experiences. In the following section you will be able to observe a number of examples of this type of self-dialogue.

The process of reflective practice

Here is another extract from *Winnie the Pooh*.

> (Pooh) had just come to the bridge; and not looking where he was going, he tripped over something and the fir-cone jerked out of his paw into the river. 'Bother', said Pooh as it floated slowly under the bridge, and he went back to get another fir-cone ... But then he thought that he would just look at the river instead, ... so he lay down and looked at it, and it slipped slowly away beneath him, ... and suddenly there was his fir-cone slipping away too. 'That's funny' said Pooh. 'I dropped it on the other side and it came out on this side! I wonder if it would do it again?' And he went back for some more fir-cones. It did. It kept on doing it. Then he dropped two in at once, and leant over the bridge to see which of them would come out first; and one of them did; but ... they were both the same size ... so the next time he dropped one big one and one little one and the big one came out first ... and he went home for tea.
>
> (Milne, 2002, p 386)

Critical thinking activity

» *Why might the above extract be said to illustrate reflection?*

One helpful way to understand reflective practice is to think of it as a process, one that Peter Tarrant suggests should be viewed as *a person trying to make sense of their own learning and wanting to make things better* (Tarrant, 2013, p 13). In the following examples this process is illustrated through the words of four teachers.

CASE STUDIES

Syed, mathematics teacher, FE college

Mark had arrived late for class again – he'd already been late more than once without giving an explanation or an apology. I wondered whether I should have said something the first time or even the second time it happened. More importantly, was it too late to tackle him now?

Should I speak to him and if so when? Should I wait until the next time he was late and say something in front of the others, before he made it to his seat? Or should I wait until he was on his own?

I decided to take the bull by the horns and have a word at the first opportunity, whatever it was, which as it happened was almost immediately, as I stumbled on him sitting by himself in the café enjoying a coffee. He was fine when I explained the problem. He told me he finds it hard to get going in the morning but he'll try. And to be honest he's not done too badly, so I'll try the 'having a quiet word' approach again.

Francesca, Spanish teacher, prison service

The PowerPoint didn't work when I switched it on. It was frustrating as it had worked perfectly well when I'd used it before. In the end I had to switch everything off and start again, when thankfully it was OK, but I had to rush the presentation through because of the delay in getting started.

Afterwards I tried to work out why it didn't work the first time. Could it have been the way I set up the equipment? I remembered that I'd set up in a bit of a rush as I knew I'd be tight for time and I wondered whether this might be the reason for the problem. So when I had a spare ten minutes I played around with the equipment and discovered that you need to plug everything in and turn the different bits on in the right order otherwise it throws a wobbly. It's been OK since then so I'll make sure I give myself time to set up properly in future.

Vincent, health and safety instructor, private training agency

It was the morning session of a workshop that I would be repeating to another group in the afternoon. I'd planned a group discussion activity. There were about 35 in the group, quite a lot so I split them into five groups. I let them get on with it and I thought things were going well as I could hear lots of discussion. But after a while it became pretty obvious that in two of the groups the discussion was dominated by a couple of people. By this time we were nearing the end of the activity so it was too late to do anything.

Over the lunch period I tried to work out why this had happened. I wondered, was it because I'd made the groups too large? Perhaps some people were reluctant to voice their views in a large group, or they may just have been put off by the more vocal ones. I wondered whether it might be worth making the groups smaller and seeing what happened. So for the afternoon session I went for eight groups in place of five. Logistically it was more difficult – the groups were a bit squashed together as space was tight, but I think it was worth it as in these smaller groups everyone appeared to make a contribution to the discussion. I was surprised but very pleased with the difference it made so I need to think carefully about group sizes in future.

Alison, employment skills, community education centre

I was congratulating myself on how well the morning session had gone and I tried to work out what it was that had made this session such a good one. It was difficult to pinpoint exactly but I think it was the atmosphere. It seemed more co-operative and friendly. But then I had to ask myself what had made the difference and I was surprised when I worked out what had been different about that morning. Sophie had come in full of news about how she was running to raise money for a local charity and she related it all to me as soon as she saw me. She was just about to repeat it to her friend when I suggested she take a few minutes to tell everyone in the class. They were all very supportive and interested in how she'd got on. As it seemed to have such a positive effect on the whole group, if time allowed, it might be worth spending a few minutes at the beginning of every session doing something similar.

Stages in the process

Each of the case studies above illustrates a four-step process. These steps are:

1. critically reflecting on an experience;

2. working out what to do differently next time;

3. trying out your ideas in practice;

4. evaluating how those ideas worked out in practice.

Critically reflecting on an experience

Reflecting on an experience from practice is at the heart of the reflective process and the conversations you have with yourself are central to it. So what form should they take? The examples give a lead. Each of the teachers begins by describing as clearly and succinctly as possible what actually happened. For example, Syed tells how Mark had arrived late for class again and Francesca relates how the PowerPoint did not work when she switched it on. This descriptive element is the most straightforward and easiest part of the conversation and so there can be a temptation to remain in descriptive mode and fail to engage in critical reflection. Yet just describing an event is not enough. Moon suggests that we:

> *… reflect on something in order to consider it in more detail … reflection appears to suggest more processing than would occur when simply recalling something.*
>
> (Moon, 2003, p 4)

Reflection moves from descriptive into critical when you try to make sense of what you have just described and to look for reasons to explain why things turned out the way they did. Having described what happened, the teachers in the case studies began to search around for ways to make sense of their experience '*I tried to work out why this had happened*'. They began to ask themselves some questions '*Could it have been the way I set up the equipment?*' and '*I wondered, was it because I'd made the groups too large?*'

Working out what to do differently next time

Having identified some possible reasons to explain what happened, the teachers in the case studies were then better equipped to work out what they might do differently next time.

Sometimes the solution presented itself easily. Vincent decided to make his groups smaller and see what happened and Francesca discovered that '*you need to plug everything in and turn the different bits on in the right order otherwise it throws a wobbly*'.

At other times the solution is tricky, or there are a number of possible options and you have to choose from them. Syed considers five different options before deciding what to do about Mark's lateness. It is not necessarily always a case of looking for a solution to a problem. It can, as shown in Alison's reflections, be about identifying how best to develop something that is working well. In any event, as is shown in all of the examples, working out what to do differently next time is about looking to improve practice.

Trying out your ideas in practice

Having identified some possible options for future action, the teachers in these examples all put their ideas into practice, testing them out. For example, Syed decided to have a word with Mark at the first opportunity and did so over a cup of coffee, while Vincent reorganised his class into eight groups in place of five for the afternoon session.

Evaluating how your ideas worked out in practice

Having tried out their ideas, each of the teachers commented on how well they had stood up to the test. They evaluated, or made a judgement about the usefulness of their ideas; for instance Vincent says, '*I think it was worth it as, in these smaller groups, everyone appeared to make a contribution to the discussion*'. This evaluation then informed his future action '*I need to think carefully about group sizes in future*'; and similarly for Francesca: '*I'll make sure I give myself time to set up properly in future*'.

Critical thinking activity

» *Choose one (or more) of the case studies and identify where and how each of the above stages occurs.*

» *Think back to your most recent experience of reflective practice. Try to identify these steps in the process and describe each in a short paragraph. You may find it useful to get your thoughts in order by using some sort of* pro forma*, such as the one given in Appendix 1.*

Key features of reflective practice

In addition to being described as a process, reflective practice can be said to display a number of key features.

- It is cyclical.

- It is ongoing.

- It is multi-sourced.

- It is recorded.

- It is objective and logical.

- It requires an open mind and curiosity.

It is cyclical

It is easy to see reflective practice as a linear process beginning with a problem that needs a solution or a desire to extend and develop something that is working well and ending when a satisfactory outcome is achieved. But this linear description is limited. A cyclical label better describes what is involved: a continuous process of reflection, action, more reflection and revised action ad infinitum. This can be illustrated diagrammatically (Figure 2.1).

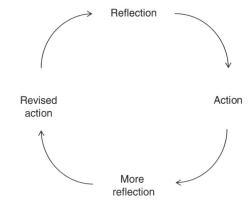

Figure 2.1 *The cyclical nature of reflective practice*

It is ongoing

If it is tempting to view reflective practice as a linear process, it is probably even easier to see it as something that you do at the beginning of your professional career and stop doing once you gain some experience. But this is not the case. On the contrary it is ongoing, becoming an almost instinctive tool in your professional practice toolkit, used throughout your career and developing as you gain experience. The aim is a continuing improvement in understanding and practice resulting in more effective teaching.

It is multi-sourced

Developing your skills as a reflective practitioner means searching for answers from more than one source. Research online and in libraries are both important sources of learning as is getting feedback from others – colleagues, mentors, line managers and your learners. In addition, you will increasingly draw on your own practical experience and knowledge as your career progresses.

It is recorded

The case studies you have observed so far in this chapter have been in the form of teachers talking about their experiences of reflective practice. Yet unless the experience is captured in a regular and systematic way, typically in the form of a reflective journal, it is likely that what you have learned will be lost.

In just the same way as in the examples of teachers talking, your journal will describe what happened, your thoughts on why it happened, your ideas for what you might do differently and what actually happened when you put your ideas into action. This can be done in a number of ways. You may prefer to write an unstructured narrative to let your thoughts flow freely. Alternatively, you could use the journal entry sheet, such as the one in Appendix 2, with specific sections to act as an aide memoire and ensure that you do not miss things out. The format of your journal is not important. What matters is that it becomes a regular, almost instinctive activity, as much a part of your practice as planning your lessons.

It is objective and logical

If undertaken systematically and logically, the reflective process will be effective in helping you to develop your teaching. Allied to this is a stepping back to observe objectively and dispassionately what is actually happening. This is not always easy to do and is particularly difficult, as you will see in later chapters, when values are challenged and/or when feelings are engaged. Yet stepping back and observing objectively is just a skill and like any other skill will develop and become easier the more you do it.

It requires an open mind and curiosity

Approaching reflective practice with as few assumptions or expectations as possible and being prepared to consider a variety of options gives you increased opportunities for learning from it. Hand in hand with this uncluttered or open-minded approach is a sense of curiosity, a desire to learn and to discover.

> *Actively engage your professional curiosity again ... Children often go through a stage when their curiosity about life is apparent. As we grow older we tend to lose the skill of asking meaningful questions. You need to redevelop your professional curiosity.*

> (Hitching, 2008, p 9)

Critical thinking activity

»   *Choose an incident from your recent teaching experience that you have reflected on and analyse your reflections in the context of the six key features that have been described above. To what extent does your reflection illustrate these features?*

Reflective practice: an illustration

The following illustration of reflective practice is taken from the journal of a teacher at the beginning of his career. As you read through the extracts, consider the extent to which they illustrate the features and process of good reflective practice.

CASE STUDY

William: reflecting on giving a project briefing

William is studying for the Certificate in Education and Training. In these early extracts from his reflective journal, William is focusing on how he presented material to his learners using PowerPoint.

Extract one

In this session I had been thinking about how well I managed to brief my group using PowerPoint slides to get the main points over. First, I got their attention, made sure they were all looking at the screen before I began. It took a few minutes because some of them were still talking and Jody and Holly had only just arrived and were fiddling around getting their stuff ready, but we got there in the end. I went through each slide carefully, speaking clearly, pausing to look round and make sure they were all still with me. I explained some of the more technical words.

After explaining each slide I looked around the group and asked whether there was anything they didn't understand or whether they had any questions. They didn't, so I carried on to the end. I then checked that everyone had understood by asking them if they knew what they needed to do next. I told them that if anyone wasn't sure they must come and have a word with me before the end of the morning. I told them that I would like them to make a start over the coming week and then we would have a review session to see how they were doing. I felt it went pretty well and we got on with the rest of the session.

This extract is essentially a factual description of what William was concentrating on and how he tried to put his thoughts into action. As yet the extract does not contain anything that can be described as *critically reflecting on an experience,* the first stage in the four-step process of reflective practice. There is no awareness of possible problems, no questioning, no thought about what he could possibly have done better.

CASE STUDY

William: reflecting on giving a project briefing

William was unexpectedly disappointed when he met the class next time to review their progress. He continues his journal entry.

Extract two

I was in for a surprise, and not a very nice one when it got to the review. When I began to look at what they'd done it was pretty obvious that something had gone very wrong. I don't think one of them had done what they were supposed to do. I couldn't believe it. What was the point of spending all that time going through the briefing if they hadn't even bothered to take any notice?

I was well irritated although I hope it didn't show too much, because at the back of my mind there was this niggling feeling that it might have been less to do with them not taking notice and more to do with something I'd done or not done. This became pretty clear when a couple of them had a good moan at me saying they'd forgotten what to do but they wouldn't have done it wrong if I'd given them the stuff that was on the PowerPoint as a handout. It was obvious – how stupid could I have been? Simple – next time give them a handout.

Critical thinking activity

» *Would you say this second extract is in any way different from the first, and if so, in what way?*

Most of this extract contains further factual description of what happened, plus a certain amount of William venting his frustration that things had gone so wrong after all his hard work planning the briefing session. He has not yet begun to search for reasons as to why things had gone wrong, yet he is perceptive enough to realise that it is more likely to be connected to something he has done, or not done, rather than his learners – the first signs here of reflecting critically. William is then handed some important information on a plate when a couple of his learners tell him they would have benefited from a handout. To his credit, despite feeling disappointed and frustrated, William catches on immediately. He has been given an explanation of why his learners had got it wrong and was open-minded enough to accept the criticism and put it right next time: '*It was obvious – how stupid could I have been? Simple – next time give them a handout*'. He continues his journal entry.

CASE STUDY

William: reflecting on giving a project briefing

Extract three

The next time I needed to brief my group I made sure it was backed up with a handout. Thankfully there was no repeat performance of the earlier fiasco – most of them had got it right, although there were still more of them than I would have wished who hadn't done what they were supposed to do. But on the whole I was pretty relieved and pleased. Later I was trying to puzzle out why a few had still got it wrong. Had they not understood the handout? Had they even bothered to read it? Had they lost it? I had to think of a way of making the information stay in their heads. Perhaps at the end of the briefing before I give them the handout I could try asking them to tell me exactly what they needed to do instead of just asking whether they understood. And perhaps I might be able to allocate a little time for them to share their ideas of how they were going to tackle it with the class. I'm definitely going to try that out.

Critical thinking activity

» *How would you evaluate this final extract from William's journal? Consider to what extent it illustrates the process and features of reflective practice.*

In this third extract, William is testing out the idea of backing up his briefing with a handout. He then makes a judgement as to its success and on the whole is relieved and pleased. He could have left it there. After all, most of his learners had got it right. But he does not. He wants things to be even better. So he starts to ask why? The answers to the *why* question lead him to think of a couple of possible things he could try out.

William's final extract is a much better example of reflective practice. Here you can see him working through the steps of the reflective practice process. He has selected an issue: the fact that some of his learners had still not understood the task he had set them. Then he begins to ask questions '*Why had a few still got it wrong?*' and to search for possible reasons: *critically reflecting on the experience*. He has worked out some possible solutions – more focused questioning and allocating more time: *working out what to do differently next time*. Finally he has resolved to try these tactics out: *trying out ideas in practice*. If he continues to reflect after the next lesson he will have completed the cycle: *evaluating how ideas worked out in practice*. The cycle can start again with more reflection and revised action.

You can also identify the main features of reflective practice from this journal extract. Firstly, William learns from his learners and from his own reflective thinking: *multi-sourced*. Secondly, he steps back to examine the situation and searches for answers: *objective and logical*. Thirdly, he is open to his learners' complaint about the lack of a handout and continues to search for solutions: *open-minded and curious*. Finally, he is involved in a continuous process of action, reflection, revised action, more reflection and more action: *cyclical and ongoing*. And, of course, it is all *recorded* in his journal.

The process you have observed in the case studies in this chapter is often illustrated in the form of a model. Kolb's (1983) model of learning through experience is a good example. Figure 2.2 shows how he envisaged the process.

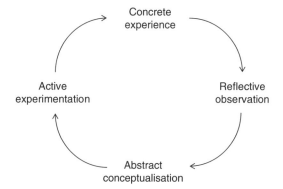

Figure 2.2 *Kolb's four stage learning cycle*

In relation to reflective practice, these stages of the learning cycle can be expressed in simpler terms as follows:

- concrete experience: doing something;

- reflective observation: thinking about it;

- abstract conceptualisation: searching for answers;

- active experimentation: trying out your ideas.

Models of reflective practice can be helpful in focusing your mind on the steps involved when you are engaged in reflective practice. Like all theory, models are there to aid understanding. Not everyone finds them easy but they are worth persevering with and keeping in mind when you are engaged in reflective practice.

Critical thinking activity

» *How useful would you find Kolb's model for exploring Pooh's actions in the extract earlier in the chapter. Identify evidence of Pooh using concrete experience, reflective observation, abstract conceptualisation and active experimentation.*

Conclusion

In this chapter you have been introduced to some of the key themes of reflective practice and observed how professionals from different spheres reflect. You have looked at possible opportunities to begin reflecting on your own practice; you have been introduced to the steps involved in the process of reflection and explored some of its key features.

In the following chapters you will see how the ideas and themes introduced here are developed and expanded when applied to practical teaching situations, to developing increased self-awareness, to your relationships with your learners and your colleagues and to continuing professional development.

Chapter reflections

» *Teachers reflect in different ways depending on the situation and the stage they have reached in their professional life. It is important to find your own ways to reflect.*

» *Reflective practice can be understood as a process involving a number of identifiable steps.*

» *Reflective practice is ongoing, cyclical, multi-sourced, recorded, objective, logical and requires an open mind and a sense of curiosity.*

Taking it further

Roffey-Barentsen, J and Malthouse, R (2009) *Reflective Practice in the Lifelong Learning Sector.* Exeter: Learning Matters.

This book provides a straightforward approach to reflective practice with a mixture of theory, practical examples and tasks.

Hillier, Y (2002) *Reflective Teaching in Further and Adult Education.* London: Continuum.

Hillier offers a more in-depth study of reflective practice, with reference to practical teaching. It also explores developments in the United Kingdom and in Europe.

References

Dewey, J (1933) *How We Think*. Chicago: Henry Regnery.

Ghaye, A and Ghaye, K (1998) *Teaching and Learning through Critical Reflective Practice*. London: David Fulton Publishers.

Hitching, J (2008) *Maintaining Your Licence to Practice*. Exeter: Learning Matters.

Kolb, D (1983) *Experiential Learning*. Englewood Cliffs, NJ: Prentice-Hall.

Milne, AA (2002) *Winnie the Pooh Complete Story Collection*. London: Egmont Books Ltd.

Moon, J (2003) *Reflection in Learning & Professional Development*. London: Kogan Page Ltd.

Tarrant, P (2013) *Reflective Practice and Professional Development*. London: Sage.

Warnock, M (1998) *An Intelligent Person's Guide to Ethics*. London: Gerald Duckworth & Co Ltd.

3 Reflecting on practical teaching issues

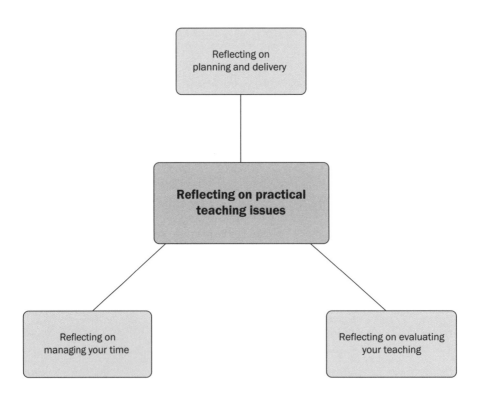

Chapter aims

This chapter will help you to:

*   understand the role of reflective practice in planning, delivering and evaluating your teaching;

*   apply the principles of reflective practice to your teaching;

*   reflect on how to manage your time effectively.

Introduction

You have now been introduced to some of the key themes of reflective practice. These themes are developed and expanded in this and the following three chapters. Although concerned with the practicalities of teaching, this chapter is not primarily about teaching skills. Rather the emphasis is on critical reflection as a key skill of effective professional teaching. The chapter focuses initially on reflecting on planning and delivery, before moving on to reflecting on evaluating your teaching. The final section of the chapter is about reflecting on time management issues, exploring the impact of our actions on colleagues, learners and others.

Reflecting on planning and delivery

Most teachers have very busy schedules and it may initially seem counter-productive to spend precious time reflecting on planning. After all, if it is not planned properly you will soon find out anyway because it is not going to work properly. While this is certainly the case, this situation is not great for the learners who are on the receiving end. Nor is there any guarantee that you will be able to deal effectively with the end results because you may not recognise that the source of the problem is to do with planning. It is all too easy to start searching for the cause of the problem in your delivery technique instead, and so begin to question your teaching ability. Reflecting on planning is worth the time you invest in it, helping to ensure that both you and your learners experience fewer hitches and more successes.

This aspect of reflection is illustrated in the following case study where an inexperienced but dedicated and enthusiastic teacher is searching for ways to improve his practice.

CASE STUDY

Leo: reflecting on planning and delivery

Leo teaches the First Diploma in Business to a lively group of learners. This is the first time he has taught this subject; it is two weeks into the course and he is reflecting in his journal on a lesson he has just taught on product promotion. Leo begins his journal entry by describing what he planned to do for the session and organising it the way he did. He then continues by describing what actually happened in the session, how he feels about how the session went and how successful his planning decisions had been.

Extract one

In the previous session I had given them some ideas on how they might set about promoting a product of their choice and I'd shown them a short film. It had gone down well and afterwards there was some useful discussion about it. We'd also talked a fair bit about the action plan I wanted them to work on for this session. So to begin this session I decided on a short discussion about logos and then, to catch their imagination, I thought of a logo contest, a sort of variation on the Eurovision Song Contest.

I'd downloaded some product logos on to the smart board. Each of my learners would have a number of points that they could allocate to the logos they thought were the best. I planned for them to come out to the front in turn to allocate their points and give their reasons for their choices. I felt this could be a mini presentation: I could observe and assess their verbal skills and it would be good preparation for the presentations proper they would be doing later. And allocating the points would be an opportunity to include some numeracy skills. Then once they'd decided on a product they could start on their action plans.

The discussion went down well and just about everyone got involved so that was good. They all liked the idea of the contest, apart from Alex who thought it was silly. But they took ages to agree on how many points they should have to allocate. In the end it was decided to go with ten as they felt this would be the easiest number to work with. Alex said she didn't want to join in and that she would start on her action plan instead.

Once the contest got started it worked reasonably well although there were some minor problems. Jack came out first, said the barest minimum and was back in his seat in double quick time – then Rihanna came out and went on and on – I had to stop her in the end. So I had to think quickly and decided that the best course of action was to give them a minimum/ maximum time limit, at least two minutes but no more than four. This worked better and on the whole the rest of the contest worked reasonably well, although I had to postpone the assessment because I got the feeling that some of them weren't taking it seriously enough.

Choosing a product also proved to be more time consuming than I'd thought. Too many of them couldn't make up their minds despite suggestions from me, and George still hadn't got anything down on paper by the end of the lesson. Because we were so behind, the action plans got squeezed out and I had to tell them to do them at home. This is far from ideal, as I can't now monitor them and give help where it is needed. In fact I feel pretty bad about getting so behind especially as it means leaving them to do the action plans on their own. I now think I should have planned the session better, but I thought I had planned it. I have another group to teach the same topic to at the end of the week so I need to get it sorted out.

Critical thinking activity

» *To what extent would you say that Leo is reflecting critically in this extract?*

» *What planning issues can you identify? Compare your response to Leo's comments given in the following extract.*

CASE STUDY

Leo: reflecting on planning and delivery

Extract two

I know I've got to put how I feel to one side and try to look at things objectively. I know that some things in this session worked really well – the discussion for a start and I'm also convinced that the logo contest was a good idea despite the problems I had. And I think I had the problems because there wasn't enough time to do the contest or for them to choose a product. I'm also unhappy that some of them didn't take things seriously enough. And I'm worried about Alex working on her action plan instead of joining in the competition. Did she really think it was silly or could there be another reason – perhaps it was the speaking out and standing in front of the class, or perhaps she was right – perhaps the contest was a bit silly after all, or maybe a bit ambitious – I just don't know.

While Leo's first journal extract is predominantly descriptive, in this second extract he begins to move from descriptive into critical reflection as he searches for the cause of the problems he experienced. Leo is feeling disheartened but has managed to step back and reflect objectively on what happened and this has allowed him to identify three planning issues that need to be sorted.

1. Timing

    •   There is too much to do in too short a time.

2. Detail

    •   The contest had not been planned in sufficient detail: for example, how much time each learner would have to explain their choice of logo.

    •   The details of how the learners would be briefed on the assessment had not been thought through; hence some did not take it seriously.

3. Inclusion

    •   One of Leo's learners had not engaged in the activity he had planned.

Leo is not sure yet what to do. He is not even certain at this stage how he feels about Alex not joining in and is now beginning to doubt his decision to include a contest in the planning for this session.

Critical thinking activity

»   *What solutions might Leo find to solve his planning and delivery problems? Compare your response to Leo's comments given in the following extract.*

CASE STUDY

Leo: reflecting on planning and delivery

Extract three

OK, so how can I improve my planning? Number one, timing – could I allow more time in my lesson planning for them to complete these activities. But we are a bit tight for time. Perhaps instead I could shorten one of the activities, probably the contest, by not letting them choose how many points – just tell them how many they were going to be given. In fact, this might be a better idea anyway as I could tell them they have say, 35 or even more points to allocate however they wish, a bit more involved than 10 so they'd have to think a bit more. And the same with choosing a product – instead of leaving them to think up a product we could have a lucky dip product bag and they'd pick from that.

Both of these changes would save time. So I need to revise my lesson plan to include details of these changes. One thing is for sure – I reckon some of them didn't take things seriously enough because I hadn't explained properly what was going to happen, especially about the assessment. And I didn't explain properly because I hadn't planned it in sufficient detail. So I'm going to make my lesson plan more detailed. I hope this will mean the contest will be worth doing for my next group – I think it will and I'd like to give it a go. I feel a bit better having sorted that lot out but I still don't know what to do about Alex.

In this third extract Leo is continuing to reflect critically on the issues he has identified. He continues to ask questions and to search for solutions, coming up with strategies that could potentially solve some of the problems. Firstly, the timing issues: planning a product lucky dip, presenting the learners with a fait accompli of points to allocate and setting time limits for speaking. Secondly, the issues of detail: Leo knows he needs to explain the purpose of the contest and the assessment to the learners in greater detail and so this needs to be planned beforehand and included in the lesson plan. He can use these strategies for his next group and in future situations so he is moving on from specifics to general, from dealing with a particular problem to planning for the future. Thirdly, inclusion: the issue of Alex not participating in the activities Leo planned has not yet been addressed and he is still uncertain how he can best support her.

Critical thinking activity

» *How might Leo find a way to support Alex? Compare your response to Leo's comments in the following extract.*

CASE STUDY

Leo: reflecting on planning and delivery

Extract four

As luck would have it I bumped into Grace, an experienced colleague in the canteen and decided to ask her about Alex. She has said on a couple of occasions she'd be glad to help if I had any worries. She told me I was right about Alex – there may well have been more to it than just thinking the contest idea was silly and yes, she could be worried about speaking in front of the others or even about the numeracy aspect. She's given me strategies which she thinks will help but just as important, she says, is being prepared, suggesting that an extra column in my lesson plan would give me a space to assess and record each of my learners' needs. In fact, I could do the same in my Schemes of Work with a space for more general notes on things like inclusion as an aid for my lesson planning.

She said it sounded like the contest had been a great idea – the learners were really involved and I should definitely use it with the other group. If I still felt doubtful I could always add in a plan B to the lesson plan, say small group work with shared tasks and a spokesperson to have just in case – apparently plan 'B's are a good idea anyway. So I'm going to make those amendments to my lesson plan. Having talked to Grace I now feel more confident about going ahead with the logo contest with my next group.

Leo continues with his journal following the session with the second group of learners.

CASE STUDY

Leo: reflecting on planning and delivery

Extract five

Well, the changes I made to my lesson plan meant my second group of learners achieved much more in the same time, so that's really good. They were just as enthusiastic about the contest and fine about being told how many points they were to have. I think that because I explained the contest and the assessment more carefully and in more detail, they had a better understanding of why they were doing it and I think it helped them to do their best. It also helped me with observing and assessing their communication skills. The product lucky dip went down well too so that was a bonus.

Afterwards most of them quickly got into the action plans and I was able to deal with any problems there and then. Some of them said they would like to design their own logos and that they could do this in their own time. In fact, I have already reversed action planning and choosing/designing a logo on my lesson plan so that I am prepared for the next time. Before they left, I asked how helpful and enjoyable they had found the lesson and on the whole they were positive although a number of them said that the handout for the action plan was pretty boring.

Reflecting on planning and delivery: conclusion

Leo's reflective journal entries highlight a number of things that are worth looking at more closely.

Objectivity

The first is the importance of stepping back to see the situation objectively. When a session does not go as it should and you are feeling negative, it is easy to become blind to every success, to go searching instead for personal failures and to lose confidence. Alternatively, and in stark contrast, there may be the temptation to gloss over a problem, to see it as just a minor hitch, something that is not important, that will sort itself out. Stepping back and looking objectively not only gives you a way of making sense of things that go wrong, it also helps to ensure that you are unlikely to become negative or to tell yourself a problem was not important. Additionally, it offers a way to acknowledge that what you are doing is good, to validate your practice and to enable you to carry on doing some of the same things with increased confidence.

Thinking on your feet

The second point of note from Leo's journal is concerned with the skill of thinking on your feet. Early on in the logo contest he realised that the contest would not work effectively as it stood. He had to think quickly and solved the problem there and then by applying a minimum and maximum time limit. The skill of thinking on your feet, the ability to think quickly and creatively, develops as you gain experience. 'Reflecting in action' is a term first put forward by Donald Schön to describe thinking on your feet. It will be explored in greater detail in later chapters.

Uncertainty

The third point illustrated in Leo's journal is that of uncertainty. Objective open-minded reflection does not always necessarily supply answers and solutions; sometimes it means living with uncertainty. An idea or an activity may become problematic, may appear less attractive, as Leo discovered when he was unsure whether to repeat the logo contest. Sometimes it takes courage to pursue an activity that you see as potentially worthwhile but risky.

Acknowledging your feelings

You may have noted that Leo's reflections included recognition of a number of feelings he experienced when he put his plan into action. For example, he records feelings of unhappiness, worry, doubt and eventually of increasing confidence. This is an important part of effective reflection, and it was emphasised by Graham Gibbs (1988) who used Kolb's model of experiential learning to develop his own theory. Gibbs' model includes a stage where your feelings about an issue are identified and taken into account when reflecting: Leo's story is a good instance of this in practice.

The value of asking for help

Another point to mention from Leo's journal is the value of asking for help when solutions do not readily present themselves, and again this can take courage. But it would be wrong to think that seeking support from a more experienced colleague means that you are in some way inadequate. A colleague can be a good sounding board: sometimes just talking about your concerns can help clarify things in your own mind. While you have been niggling over an issue, a colleague will come at it fresh and may offer new insights. In addition, as Peter Tarrant observes,

> *… feedback from other professionals enables us to take stock, to look more objectively at our practice and to consider ways of enhancing and improving what we do.*

> (Tarrant, 2013, p 97)

Reflection as a continuous activity

Finally, you would have observed from the case study that Leo engaged in a cycle of reflective practice where he recorded what happened, his thoughts and feelings about it, what was good and not so good. He tried to make sense of what happened, asked himself what else he might have done, planned what he would do differently next time, recorded in his journal what happened and his thoughts and feelings when he put his plan into action. The cycle continued with Leo looking to develop his practice through ongoing reflection and action.

Critical thinking activity

Reflect on how you feel when things do not go according to plan. You might find the following questions helpful.

» *To what extent are you likely to feel negative at what you see are failures or to gloss over a problem or issue?*

» *How easy do you find it to step back and observe your teaching objectively?*

» *How easy do you find it to ask for help from a colleague?*

Reflecting on evaluating your teaching

It is easy when you are in the thick of things, planning programmes and lessons, teaching and assessing learners, giving feedback and so on, to forget to stop and take stock, to reflect more generally on your teaching, to consider such questions as, '*What is my teaching like, why is it like this, what are the effects of my teaching on my learners?*' (Ghaye and Ghaye, 1998, p 20). Yet to find the answer to one further question that Ghaye and Ghaye pose – '*How can I improve what I do?*' – it is necessary to evaluate your teaching and to evaluate the experience of your learners. To illustrate how this evaluation might work out in practice, take another look at Leo to see how he sets about the task.

CASE STUDY

Leo: reflecting on evaluating

I have been re-reading one of my teaching text books and it's made me realise that most of what I have written in my journal so far has been about improving my practice by focusing on problems and searching for solutions. And I know that's good but I know I also need to evaluate my teaching and my learners' learning in a more structured way. I need to plan ahead more effectively and to do that I have to find answers to some more general questions. So I made myself a list of questions to think about.

- *Did I meet all my learners' needs?*

- *Did the learners learn/achieve?*

- *Were my teaching methods appropriate?*

- *Were my resources appropriate?*

- *Were my learners motivated and enjoying their learning?*

- *Did they understand how and why they were being assessed?*

- *How can I improve my teaching?*

I can answer some of the questions right away: 'Were my resources appropriate?' The answer must be no – some of my learners said the handout for the action planning was boring. I've already looked at it and they do have a point. It could do with brightening up, so that's next on my list. I was lucky to get that feedback from them, but just asking them how helpful and enjoyable they found the lesson is clearly not going to be that useful to me for evaluating my teaching. Much better I think would be to put together a simple questionnaire that asks specific questions about the usefulness of a number of different activities they have engaged in during a session.

I can also answer the question, 'Did the learners learn/achieve?' Because of the revisions I made to my lesson plan the second group got well into their action plans, so yes they did learn and achieve. The improved lesson plan also meant they had a much better understanding of how and why they were being assessed. I think this helped them to achieve the outcomes I'd set. I think it would help when I am planning my lessons to add the list of general questions into the plan. This will act as a reminder to help me keep these ideas in mind when I am teaching.

Leo has learned that structured self-dialogue, recorded in a journal, is one effective way to evaluate his teaching and his learners' learning. He has also utilised his learners' achievement as an indication of the effectiveness of his planning and teaching practice. In addition, he knows that feedback from his learners will provide him with information that will assist in evaluating his teaching.

In addition to feedback from learners, feedback from colleagues, mentors and employers can also be utilised to aid evaluation. Another effective method is the feedback that follows an observation of your teaching by a colleague or a mentor. Being observed as you teach is not the most comfortable of experiences, as you will undoubtedly know already if you are working towards QTLS or, if you are a qualified teacher, you may have some less than positive memories from being observed in the past. Yet, it is well worth the discomfort involved because another professional can pick up on things you might normally never notice, and provide you with ideas for your ongoing action plan. Another professional can also highlight your strengths, pointing out those things that you are doing well.

Critical thinking activity

» *Think about a recent occasion when you reflected to evaluate your teaching and your learners' learning? What methods did you use? What other methods might you find helpful?*

Reflecting on managing your time

One of the most difficult organisational issues that you are likely to face in FE today is that of managing your time. There never seems to be enough of it. With a busy schedule you may be reluctant to allocate time to reflect. Yet the rewards are well worth the time investment, not just in terms of saving you time in the long run, but also in making your working day easier and your relationships with those around you more positive. Just how you might set about reflecting on managing your time is illustrated in the following case study.

CASE STUDY

Mo: reflecting on managing time

Mo is a teacher who cares about her learners and who is able to enthuse and motivate them to achieve. But Mo is finding the demands of her job at a busy training agency hard going. She meets Raju, a friend and colleague, after work and starts to unload her frustrations.

'What a week – I'm exhausted! I've had nothing but hassle. Take today – I planned to get stuck in to that report for the briefing meeting next week. I only had a short teaching slot this morning and another later in the afternoon with space in the middle where I could put some time in on the report. But no such luck – every time I tried to start work, something, or someone got in the way.

To begin with I arrived back at the office after the end of the morning session to find three phone messages and a pile of letters on my desk awaiting my attention. I was just about to deal with these when a worried looking Jade from my Year 1 group appeared asking if she could have a word. She's got behind with her rent and her landlord is making things difficult. Apparently she's been giving the rent money to her boyfriend who's now dumped her. After we had a chat I took her over to Student Services – an extra half hour gone!

When I returned to the office having already lost a chunk of my report-writing time, Daniel from the job centre had turned up to discuss what he's going to do with my leavers next week. He said he'd emailed yesterday to confirm but I hadn't yet had a chance to check my emails. I managed to get things sorted with Daniel as quickly as possible although Sarah from marketing rang just as we were finishing off, asking me if I could pop over to have a look at the draft of the new brochure.

Having sorted Sarah out I grabbed a belated coffee and sandwich from the corner shop, thinking I could eat and work. But no, on getting back to the office and picking up the first of my phone messages I got a very irate Fiona asking me where I was and why wasn't I at the planning meeting. She'd emailed me two days ago informing me of the change of day and in addition, had sent a reminder by hand this morning. I could just see it now, half hidden under the pile of stuff on my desk. The rest of the phone messages had to wait.

Clutching my sandwich and coffee I made a quick dash to the planning meeting, en route preparing my apology and attempting to think of some sort of an explanation for why I had done no preparation. Pointless really – I knew I should have done it but I just hadn't managed to get round to it. Needless to say, the meeting was embarrassing. And then of course, it was time for my afternoon class and nothing done on the report. So Raju, how am I going to manage, in all this mess, to get this report done?'

Expecting sympathy from Raju, Mo was surprised and dismayed when he told her that the answer was in her own hands; that she needed to allocate some time to think about how to be more organised. Only just stifling a wail of protest Mo quickly points out that she does not *have* any time – she cannot even get the blasted report done. But Raju only repeats what he already said, adding that her chaotic approach sometimes makes life difficult for everyone else.

Making her way home after the disappointing meeting with Raju, Mo is thinking that it is OK for him, he does not have her hassle and anyway she wants to forget about work for the weekend. But Mo cannot seem to forget what Raju said about making life difficult for everyone else and wonders if perhaps he has a point. She has not been in control of events. She is disorganised and for much of the time she reacts to other people's agendas instead of setting her own. What might it be like, she wonders, for her colleagues to have to work with someone who does not answer emails regularly and who arrives late and unprepared for meetings?

Then her thoughts turned to her learners – she got behind with their project reports the other week and they had to wait for their feedback and she has, on more than one occasion, arrived in class without the handouts for the session because she had not been able to find them among the mess that comprises her desk-top filing system. Mo knows she is a good teacher but realises she needs to allocate time over the weekend to thinking seriously about managing her time, otherwise she is going to continue to struggle and her colleagues and learners will get fed up with her. But where to start?

Critical thinking activity

» *How might Mo initiate a process of reflection aimed at improving her time management skills? Compare your response to the continuation of the case study below.*

CASE STUDY

Mo's story continued

Mo begins her reflective task by writing down the things that had directly or indirectly prevented her from getting on with the report. Her list included: allowing others to interrupt her – Jade and Sarah; not checking her emails on a regular basis; not checking her phone messages on a regular basis; keeping her desk in a mess and, she reluctantly admits, procrastinating over writing the report. Reading through her list Mo can now see that identifying some of the reasons for her chaos provides her with some potential solutions. For example, allocate a regular time to check phone and email messages and stick to it, tidy her desk and work out a proper filing system, make a list of the things she needs to do and so on. Then she comes to a full stop: she's run out of ideas.

Mo then turns to the internet to search for time management strategies and is pleased to discover that making a list of tasks is a good first step. And she is not disappointed with what else she finds out. She learns that her tasks need to be prioritised. She also discovers techniques to help with scheduling her time, completing tasks, dealing with interruptions and setting up a filing system. She even finds out how to deal with procrastination – divide big tasks into small chunks.

Over the weekend, working with a concept map, Mo begins to form an action plan. She then starts to put her plan into action. First she clears and tidies her email account. Then she draws up a schedule of tasks that she wishes to accomplish during the following week, making sure the most important and urgent ones are dealt with first. She is starting to feel more in control, more positive and can even look forward to Monday morning. She knows it is going to take a while before the time management techniques are all in place and up and running but she knows she has her action plan at hand to keep her focused.

Critical thinking activity

» *Return to Kolb's model of experiential learning described in the previous chapter and apply it to Mo's experience. How useful do you find it for providing a framework for Mo's process of reflective practice?*

You probably had little difficulty in identifying the four stages of Kolb's model in this case study. Clearly Mo had an abundance of concrete experience, and very stressful it was too. Prompted by Raju, she found time to reflect on what had happened and to search for answers. Finally, she began to try out her new ideas about how to manage her time more effectively.

There are some useful things to be drawn from Mo's experience. Her weekend of reflecting has given her a number of insights. One of the most valuable has been an awareness of the impact of her actions on her colleagues and her learners. This is a major step for any-one engaged in reflective practice, to cross the metaphorical bridge and view events from someone else's perspective. Notwithstanding Mo's reflective leap, there is nothing evident in either her conversation with Raju or her reflective practice that she is or has been aware of the effect of her disorganised behaviour on herself. Yet clearly she is affected and clearly has suffered.

Much of the frustration and exhaustion that Mo has been experiencing has been a direct consequence of her own actions. With the help of Raju who has been the catalyst for her reflective practice, Mo has been able to work out how she can make positive changes to her professional practice. What she has not yet realised is that once she is able to be more organised, her professional working day will be more enjoyable and her relationships with others easier and more positive. The practical changes she has already begun to make will also affect her colleagues and for the better. In the long run, though, it is going to be her learners who will gain, because no matter how good the teaching, if a teacher is disorganised it will ultimately be the learners who suffer most.

You may well be in a similar work situation to Mo where everyone wants a piece of your time and you are constantly being interrupted as you try to do a professional job. Teaching has always been a demanding profession and the administrative pressures on all staff are now substantial. These pressures take their toll; like Mo you may well be feeling overburdened, exhausted and stressed. Yet these pressures also make it even more necessary to be as organised as you can, to manage and make best use of your time. When under pressure it can be difficult to lift your head above the water; you are too busy firefighting. Yet reflecting critically and objectively about how you manage your time is the way forward.

Just like other aspects of reflective teaching, the process will begin, as Mo discovered, with looking at your own situation and identifying specifics that you want to change or improve. You may for example find it difficult to say no to requests for your time, or you may, like Mo and most of us at some time or other, procrastinate over tasks that you know you should do but which appear huge and daunting. A big task like writing a report for example can seem unattractive and the temptation to find other things to do to avoid getting started is all too real.

The good news is that time management solutions come as a set of skills that you can learn and like all skills they improve the more you use them. Fortunately, as Mo discovered, you can easily access information and techniques on how to schedule your tasks, deal with inter-ruptions and so on. These will assist you to draw up an action plan that you can then put into practice and evaluate. In addition to information online, there are lots of books that can help – see 'Taking it further' at the end of the chapter – as well as the help that may be avail-able from your colleagues and/or provided by your organisation.

There will always be frustrations and it is never possible to completely avoid firefighting; this is the nature of teaching in FE. But taking responsibility for your own time management is the professional approach, allowing you to take control of your working day rather than it controlling you. Learning the skills of time management may take a little time: you may find yourself slipping back into old ways. We are creatures of habit and we know that old habits die hard. Nor do we necessarily welcome change, especially if that change is related to our behaviour. Yet it is well worth the effort because the benefits are substantial, not only for you professionally but also for those around you.

Critical thinking activity

Reflect on your own time management needs. You might find the following questions helpful.

» *How organised would you say you are?*

» *Do you prioritise your tasks?*

» *Do you always get jobs done on time?*

» *Are you always on time for meetings and classes?*

» *Is your filing system appropriate?*

» *Do you check emails and phone messages on a regular and systematic basis?*

» *Do you regularly allow others to interrupt?*

Conclusion

The focus of this chapter has been on the role of reflective practice in enhancing and developing the skills of planning, delivery, evaluation and time management. The reflective practice process has been evident in the case studies of the two teachers. You will also have observed many of the features of reflective practice; for example, it is multi-sourced, objective, ongoing and cyclical.

Yet teaching is not only about good planning and organising. It is just as much, and perhaps even more, connected to the relationships that teachers have with their learners and their colleagues. Teachers do not work in isolation and in the final part of the chapter you saw how the actions of one teacher affected those around her. Professional relationships and professional interactions are enhanced by a teacher's awareness of those things that guide their actions and the ability to communicate effectively and sensitively. Reflecting on these issues is the topic of the following chapters.

Chapter reflections

» *Stepping back to look objectively will help to avoid brushing over issues or becoming focused on perceived failures; feelings do need to be taken into account when reflecting on an issue.*

» *Reflecting in action is the ability to think quickly and creatively on your feet; it develops through experiences and practice.*

» *Reflecting can sometimes result in uncertainty. Colleagues can often provide support, giving advice, acting as a sounding board and/or observing practice.*

» *Evaluation is about taking stock and searching for answers to some general questions on how to improve practice; sources of information for evaluation include self-dialogue, learners' achievement, and feedback from learners, colleagues and others.*

» *Reflecting on time management issues and developing key skills improves relationships with learners and colleagues.*

Taking it further

Morgenstern, J (2004) *Time Management from the Inside Out*. New York: Owl Books.

This is a detailed and practical book on time management strategies. Written in a clear and logical style, it gives you ideas on how to tailor these strategies to your particular context and needs.

Wallace, S (2007) *Teaching, Tutoring and Training in the Lifelong Learning Sector*. Exeter: Learning Matters.

Susan Wallace's comprehensive and accessible book has helpful sections on reflective planning, preparation, assessment and evaluation.

References

Ghaye, A and Ghaye, K (1998) *Teaching and Learning through Critical Reflective Practice*. London: David Fulton Publishers.

Gibbs, G (1988) *Learning by Doing: A Guide to Teaching and Learning Methods*. Oxford: Oxford Polytechnic Further Education Unit.

Schön, D (2006) *The Reflective Practitioner: How Professionals Think in Action*. London: Ashgate Publishing.

Tarrant, P (2013) *Reflective Practice and Professional Development*. London: Sage.

4 Reflective practice and self-awareness

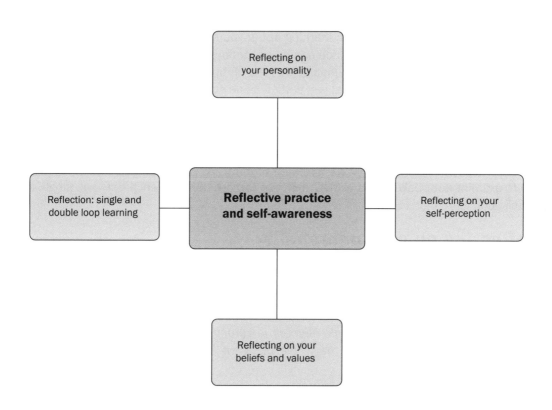

Chapter aims

This chapter will help you to:

• reflect on your personality and self-perception and how they relate to your practice;

• reflect on and value your strengths and plan how you can develop these in your practice;

• reflect on your personal beliefs and values to learn how they inform your teaching;

• recognise the difference between single and double loop learning.

Introduction

This chapter is all about reflecting on yourself. The pursuit of self-knowledge is not new: throughout history philosophers and those in search of wisdom have sought to learn more about themselves. However, for modern day individuals with busy lives there often seems to be little time for navel gazing, an activity sometimes viewed as fluffy and indulgent. Yet this could not be further from the truth; learning about yourself requires curiosity, commitment and an open mind, and the experience can be uncomfortable. And there is no doubt it does take time; for some of the ancient philosophers, a lifetime. That amount of dedication just is not possible for the majority of us; yet, setting aside some time to self-reflect is worth the effort because the insights you gain about yourself as an individual and as a teacher will enhance your teaching.

This chapter covers a number of key themes of self-awareness. Through a series of case studies it asks you to reflect on your personality and your self- perception before encouraging you to examine your beliefs and values and then explore the difference between single and double loop learning.

Reflecting on your personality

It would be a mistake to underestimate the degree to which your individual personality influences your approach to your practice, what happens in your teaching groups and your learners' responses to you. This important point has been highlighted by Jenny Rogers.

> *Your influence is the most single element in setting the style of a group: as great or even greater influence on the whole occasion than the sum of all the other individuals.*
>
> (Rogers, 2001, p 51)

With such a strong recommendation, reflecting on your personality takes on greater significance. How one teacher sets about doing this is illustrated in the following case study.

CASE STUDY

Franklin: reflecting on personality

Franklin is a physical training instructor in the armed forces. He has recently begun teaching a Vocational A level in Sports Science programme part time at his local FE college. Franklin is feeling dispirited following a particularly difficult session with his new learners. He records the experience in his journal.

Extract one

Things aren't going too well with my sports science students. I've been teaching them now for four weeks and I'm finding it hard. This morning is a good example. My usual policy is to get straight into things so that they know how much work is involved if they want a decent qualification. I had already told them that in the session today we would be starting to look at nutrition. So this morning I carefully briefed them on what they were going to be doing and what I was expecting them to achieve during the session. When I'd finished I gave them a handout with everything clearly set out, before asking them if they had any questions.

There weren't any questions so I handed out the first task, a short research project on probiotics. I put them in groups of three, small groups because I wanted to make sure no one had an opportunity to slack. I picked one person from each group to record the results of their research and handed out a number of books where they would find the relevant information. I told them they had half an hour during which time I would be visiting each group in turn to see how they were getting on.

I can't work out why they didn't seem able to just get on with it. It was straightforward enough and clearly they shouldn't have been in any doubt about what they were supposed to be doing. To be fair some of them did get on with it, probably a good half of the class but within minutes there were problems with the other half. It started with Loren taking all day to get what she needed from her bag and getting settled. Then within minutes of each other Joel and Danielle decided they needed the loo. Then when I approached the first group I found they'd done nothing – hadn't even opened a book – it was boring they said. Before I even had a chance to get them back on task an argument started in another of the groups and I had to go and sort it out.

During this fiasco the groups that had begun to get down to work were being distracted – they kept stopping to look and listen to the 'entertainment' from the dissenters. In the end I had to remind the whole class that they now had only ten minutes left and I expected a minimum of five pertinent points from each group. This seemed to do the trick and thankfully they got stuck in. But it's bothering me. I don't yet understand what caused all this but I do need to work it out.

Critical thinking activity

»   *What can you say about Franklin's personality from reading his journal extract?*

»   *What connections can you see between Franklin's personality and his learners' behaviour?*

Franklin is a dedicated teacher who wants to improve his practice so he knows he needs to reflect on what happened and more importantly why it happened. He could have been tempted to put the blame squarely on his learners, '*they're just not motivated*' or '*they were having an off day*', but he is perceptive enough to realise the reasons for their tardy responses may have other causes and he begins to reflect more creatively.

CASE STUDY

Franklin: reflecting on personality

Extract two

Going over what happened this morning I started thinking about a teacher I had when I was at school. He was great – I really liked and admired him. I was keen to do well in his classes and I wondered why? Was his approach different to mine? Then I tried to imagine him in front of my group of learners, to imagine what he would say and do. I couldn't really picture it but I think he might be more relaxed than I am. But I'm not like that. And that's not how I teach my forces students. They expect and welcome the 'this is what we are going to do and this is how we are going to do it' approach. Are my sports science learners different? Do I need to be less rigid? Should I be more collaborative? I don't think I will find it easy but perhaps it's worth trying and seeing what happens. Will it make a difference? Will each new group I have in the future need a different way of doing things? I don't know.

Perhaps a rigid approach to his teaching came naturally to Franklin, or perhaps it was a characteristic he had acquired from his military teaching experience. Either way he was brave enough to reflect critically on what happened, to question his approach and compare himself to a teacher from his school days that he had liked and admired. Reflecting critically on his personality and how it informed his teaching helped Franklin to identify some potential strategies he could use to better support his learners and indeed his future learners.

Critical thinking activity

»   *Reflect on an experience you have had where something has happened (positive or negative) which you feel was in some way connected to your personality? What can you learn from this? How can you use this knowledge to develop your teaching?*

The chances are that if you had to describe your personality you might struggle: we just do not have any facility for observing ourselves in action. Yet there are a number of tools you can use that can help you to initiate a productive reflective process.

One perhaps rather surprising strategy is drawing; creating your own *selfie*, a drawing of how you see yourself. It does not matter what you draw as long as you try to produce an honest image of how you see yourself. This can often be enlightening because drawing works in a different way to writing as it uses the right creative side of your brain rather than the left rational side and can therefore sometimes highlight something you would not think to write. You do not need to have any sort of artistic skill, stick figures work well, and if you can do this with a friend or colleague and share your thoughts, so much the better.

Getting together with someone else and asking them to give you a description of your personality is a good strategy anyway. It needs to be someone you know well where you trust their judgement and their ability to give their honest view of you. Some of the things you might want to explore are:

- whether you are more of an optimist or pessimist;
- whether you are a logical or erratic thinker;
- how determined and committed you are;
- the expectations you have of yourself;
- the extent to which you hold to your views or accept what others say;
- how well you manage stress.

Another way to gain insight into your personality is to use a questionnaire. There are numerous types and they can provide you with information on different aspects of your personality. Many of these personality questionnaires are lightweight and superficial but a number of them are robust and more in-depth. One of the best known is the Myers–Briggs Type Indicator. This psychometric questionnaire, developed from Jung's model of personality, has been used extensively in the workplace by HR departments. It assesses the following four aspects of personality.

1. The extent to which you tend towards extraversion or introversion.
2. The extent to which your perception relies on experience/senses or on intuition.
3. The extent to which your decisions are based on the logic of the situation or on feelings and values.
4. The extent to which your preferred lifestyle is based on planning or spontaneity.

The Myers-Briggs Indicator has little scientific validity and has been criticised for being oversimplified, being based on either/or choices that offer little middle ground. Despite these limitations it can be a potentially useful tool for gaining insight into some aspects of your personality.

Critical thinking activity

» *Complete the Myers–Briggs questionnaire online (you can locate it through any search engine) and make a note of what you learn. Reflect on how you might use this knowledge to develop your teaching.*

Reflecting on your personal strengths

Reflecting on your personal strengths helps you to recognise what you do best. The idea of a best self has been developed within the field of positive psychology. Psychologists Christopher Peterson and Martin Seligman (2004) highlight the value of recognising and using personal strengths in learning. They identify and classify 24 behavioural strengths that they place into six classes of core virtues. What these core virtues have in common is that they are viewed as desirable across cultures and history. Peterson and Seligman demonstrate how a variety of strengths is illustrated through the lives of famous people, for example, Albert Einstein and creativity, Ernest Shackleton and bravery, Benjamin Franklin and love of learning, Oprah Winfrey and social intelligence. Identifying and acknowledging your particular strengths provides you with an image of yourself in which you are working at your best.

Critical thinking activity

»   *Research Peterson and Seligman's classification of personal strengths online. Identify those you think have value in teaching and give reasons for your choices.*

Reflecting on your self-perception

In just the same way as your personality affects your approach to teaching and to relationships with your learners and colleagues, so too will it influence your perception of yourself. Reflecting on events from your teaching will inform your self-perception as a teacher. When just casually thinking back over events in your practice, it is easy to become overly self-critical and focus on problems and failures rather than successes. This is not good for your confidence levels. Engaging in reflective practice, on the other hand, can provide you with a more honest and balanced assessment of how you are doing. This is illustrated in the following case study where becoming a learner was the trigger for one teacher to reflect on her self-perception.

CASE STUDY

Thea: reflecting on self-perception

Thea teaches beauty therapy at her local college and is working towards the Certificate in Education and Training. Her perception of her teaching is skewed by her tendency in her reflective practice to focus on problems and failures. In the following extract from her journal, she describes how her experience of joining a local history class initiated a process of reflection that helped her to explore and then to challenge her skewed perception of herself as a teacher.

I'd enrolled on this leisure course in local history. When I arrived Guy the teacher was at the front doing something with the projector and there was an older man trying to talk to him, asking him something I think, but I don't think Guy was really listening to him. There were eight of us including me; the man trying to talk to the teacher, a women sitting near me looking down at her hands, two guys sitting fairly close together but not talking to each other and three women in the back row who obviously knew each other as they were chatting and laughing about something. I didn't know any of them and was hit by an unexpected wave of disappointment and a feeling of isolation.

As Guy was doing the final bits to the projector I turned to the woman near me and said, 'Hello, I'm Thea' and she responded with a relieved expression, a tentative smile and a timid 'I'm Tima'. I could see that she was feeling apprehensive so I suggested we sit together. We got talking and she told me that she was from Azerbaijan. She had come to the class in order to join in with local interests but she was worried about her English. She was frightened of being shown up and looking stupid because she wasn't confident in speaking. I tried to put her at ease and said I'd help if she would like me to and she seemed really pleased and keen.

Having finished fiddling with the projector Guy suggested to the man waiting to ask a question that he might like to go and sit down and then Guy introduced himself. He gave each of us a number of handouts and went through each one – I was wondering how Tima was managing. When he'd finished he put up a picture of a local church on the whiteboard and told us to work in pairs or threes and glean what we could from it. It was obvious that the three women were going to stick together and form their own group. The two guys made a reluctant semi shuffle towards each other but the older 'question' man looked a bit lost, poor guy, so I smiled at him and asked if he would like to join us two women.

I can't say Guy wasn't good at his job because he was. He was professional, gave us lots of information, was clear, well organised, everything was carefully planned and so on. But, and it's a big but, I don't think he was all that interested in us, or even in anything we had to say. He was there to do a job and I got the feeling that it wasn't all that relevant who was sitting in front of him.

This experience has got me thinking about the difference between Guy's class and mine. I think it is the atmosphere. In mine there is a community spirit – I always try to encourage everyone to share their ideas and help each other and I think everyone benefits from it.

The thing is, I hadn't really registered all this good stuff because I am always looking at the negative bits. And once you focus on the not so good things it's not easy to get them out of your mind – they go round and round in your head like one of those irritating tunes. It's not a nice place to be and there have been times when I have begun to doubt that I could ever be good at my job. Having this experience of being a learner I recognise some of the good things about my teaching and can now see that I'm better at what I do than I thought I was. Instead of always looking at the negatives I am going to focus more on my successes. So I have begun to make a list of all the positives. My next task is to work out how I can develop and extend them and use them in new ways.

Critical thinking activity

What is your opinion of yourself as a teacher? You might find the following questions helpful.

»   *How do you feel when things go wrong?*

»   *Are you able to identify the positives as well as the negatives?*

»   *How confident are you that you can enthuse and inspire your learners?*

»   *How confident are you that you can identify and manage problems and stressful situations?*

»   *What is your opinion of Thea's decision to focus on her successes?*

When problems arise or when things do not go according to plan, it is natural when reflecting afterwards to concentrate on these negative events. And as has been illustrated in earlier chapters, this is no bad thing. Kate Kennett suggests that some of our most valuable learning is drawn from reflecting on our mistakes. Yet Kennett goes on to say that *'when people make mistakes they are often overwhelmed with preoccupying emotions that are confusing if not actually negative in quality'* (Kennett, 2010, p 73). When mistakes and errors are given too much attention they can take on ogre proportions, as happened to Thea when she could not stop thinking about them even when she wanted to. But learning from our mistakes is not the only option available when reflecting to improve practice. Indeed Tony Ghaye (2010) suggests that these *'deficit-type questions'*, when the focus is on what goes wrong rather than what goes right, may not even be the best way.

> *When we focus on problems we begin to construct a world in which problems are central; they become the dominant realities that burden us ... If we ask questions about our problems and about things that we feel have gone less well than we had expected then we grow in that direction. If we ask questions about successes and fulfilment then we grow in this direction.*
>
> (Ghaye, 2010, pp 9–10)

Ghaye goes on to suggest that to become the best you can, it is important to have balance, and to reflect on the positives so that you can learn to recognise and then develop your talents and gifts. He offers three questions to ask yourself to help you to appreciate what you are really able to do.

•   *Who benefits from what you do and in what ways?*

•   *How does this make them feel and how do you know this?*

•   *How does this make you feel?*

(Ghaye, 2010, p 11)

For Thea there are positive outcomes from reflecting on her practice. The first is that she has a new, more balanced view of her teaching. The second is that having recognised the many things she does that benefit her learners she intends to continue doing them but with greater confidence. The third is she will look for opportunities to develop and expand her successes and to transfer them into future contexts.

As Thea's experience illustrated, each of us has our own individual way of thinking about ourselves. You will have your own beliefs about your efficacy, how competent, effective and successful you feel you would be in any situation that might arise. Recognising and valuing your strengths and successes increases your sense of self-efficacy and your level of self-esteem, how much you value yourself and how much you believe you are valued by others. This is important. As Zwozdiak-Myers points out, beliefs about our capabilities impact on what we do.

> *Efficacy beliefs ... have been found to underpin the choices and decisions teachers make within their roles and are considered to be a strong predictor of teacher behaviour.*
>
> (Zwozdiak-Myers, 2012, p 82)

The greater your sense of self-efficacy and level of self-esteem the more confident and the more motivated you will be and this can only benefit your learners. Reflective practice can help you to identify positives as well as negatives, providing a more balanced assessment of how you are doing.

Reflecting on your beliefs and values

The final part of the self-awareness trilogy is concerned with the personal beliefs and values that shape our lives. Beliefs and values can be listed and labelled:

> *attitudes, value judgements, axioms, opinions, ideology, perceptions, conceptions, conceptual systems, preconceptions, dispositions ... personal theories ... rules of practice ...*
>
> (Pajares, 1992, p 309, in Zwozdiak-Myers, 2012, p 83)

Beliefs and values are, on the whole, deeply rooted and often unacknowledged. Yet their role in informing our actions is significant, so it makes sense to identify and examine them in order to discover how they might influence your teaching.

Beliefs

You have already explored some of your beliefs earlier in this chapter; your beliefs about yourself and about what you can do. The focus now shifts to your beliefs about others, especially your beliefs about your learners and how these beliefs inform your teaching. The following two case studies illustrate how these beliefs can be examined and then challenged through the process of critical reflection. Read through them both before considering the next critical thinking activity.

CASE STUDIES

Gillie's beliefs

Gillie teaches a community-led creative writing course one evening a week; she has just gained the Award in Education and Training. A critical event at the end of the creative writing course compelled her to recognise, examine and reassess one of her beliefs. Here she describes the reflective process involved.

At the end of the final session I asked them to complete an evaluation questionnaire – I wanted to get some feedback on how they felt about their learning programme. Later when I read through the completed questionnaires, one of them (Geoffrey's – I recognised his handwriting) gave me a minor shock and a lot to think about. Against the question that had asked for an opinion on the teaching, Geoffrey had written that on the whole it was very good but he felt that I sometimes patronised him. At first I couldn't believe it – I am absolutely committed to inclusivity and just wouldn't patronise anyone.

But it kept nagging at me, the thought that Geoffrey felt he'd been patronised. Why did he feel this? And I couldn't help thinking about the fact that Geoffrey was a fair bit older than the rest of the group and this fact niggled. I tried to think back over the weeks of the course and it wasn't easy but I stuck at it and there were a number of things I did recall doing. The first was right at the start of the first session. I remember Geoffrey coming into the classroom and wanting to make him feel welcome and comfortable, encouraged him to come and sit at the front where he could see the board easily. Another thing I remember doing is changing the font size on my handouts from 12 to 14.

It took me a bit of time and even more soul searching to realise that when I explained something to the group I think I probably focused more of my attention on Geoffrey and I now think I gave him more attention overall. I thought I was just making him feel included; instead I was making him feel separate and patronised and I didn't even realise what I was doing. Did I feel that he should be treated differently because he was older? I must have assumed that he couldn't do well without extra help simply because he was older than the others. What else did I do? Did I have lower expectations of him? Did I assess his work differently? How can I avoid doing this in the future?

Jo's beliefs

Jo is a newly qualified teacher who teaches Science GCSE. Here he records how he learnt through the reflective process to recognise, examine and reassess his beliefs about one of his learners.

I hadn't much liked Adam right from day one. For a start he was good at boasting about what he knew or he'd done. He'd take any opportunity during class discussions to mention he knew this or had done that. I had to keep a strict eye on him in group work because he would take over and talk about himself given half a chance. And he was good at passing the buck – if something went wrong it was someone else's fault but never his. I think what irritated me most was he didn't actually bother to do any of the work I gave them. When I asked him about it he just said he'd been too busy and he'd sit there with a 'know it all but can't be bothered to say' expression. So all in all I wasn't that motivated to spend too much time on him and I sort of mentally side-lined him, feeling my time was better spent helping the others who did want to work.

But about six weeks into the term I was in town and I bumped into one of the other learners from this class. We were just chatting and I was asking her how she was enjoying the classes and she told me something in passing that got me thinking. She said that in one of the classes she'd asked Adam if he could jot down the details of an app he'd been talking about. She'd handed him a pen and paper but he'd got very flustered, handed it back and said he'd dictate the details. It had puzzled her. It puzzled me too. So on the way home I started to think about him. Why was he flustered when asked to write something? Why was he always boasting and blaming others? Why was he reluctant to hand in any work? As soon as I got in I went online and I discovered that sometimes someone with low confidence can appear arrogant or blame others. First thing next morning I had a word with Eric, a colleague with many years teaching experience, and he reckoned from what I told him that Adam might have a problem with writing.

Well Eric was correct although it turned out Adam's literacy problem wasn't too serious at all, he just found spelling difficult, but it was serious to him because he was acutely embarrassed about it and all his actions were a camouflage to prevent its discovery. I'd just assumed Adam was a pain in the neck. It makes you think though – of course I value diversity – it goes without saying and I really believe it shows in my teaching. In this case though, I reckon I allowed my beliefs about the reasons for Adam's behaviour to get in the way.

Critical thinking activity

» *What assumptions did Gillie and Jo make about their learners and what beliefs were they based on?*

» *Identify the personal qualities that Gillie and Jo needed in order to reflect critically on their beliefs about their learners.*

Through reflection Gillie and Jo were able to identify and then challenge the beliefs they had about two of their learners. For Gillie this process began with asking herself why Geoffrey might feel that he was being patronised. She saw that she had treated him differently from the other learners because she had assumed that he would need extra help, more attention and bigger print. Gillie had believed she was promoting inclusion until she recognised in herself a deep-seated, unacknowledged belief that older people find learning more difficult than younger people. Through reflection she questioned her actions and in the process challenged the beliefs that informed them.

For Jo the reflective process was different. He had assumed that Adam did not hand in any work because he could not be bothered. He believed that Adam was arrogant, lazy and self-centred and not deserving of his help and support. A chance encounter with one of his learners forced him to look for other possible reasons for Adam's behaviour, leading him to research online and then to seek advice from a more experienced colleague. Jo valued diversity and firmly believed that he was active in promoting it, but reflecting on the experience with Adam enabled him to reassess his actions and the beliefs that informed them. This relationship between self-awareness and actions has been noted. There is

> *... an immediate connection between changed awareness of assumptions unearthed through the reflective process and the changed practices that suggest themselves on the basis of these changed awarenesses.*
>
> (Fook and Gardner, 2007, p 15)

Gillie's belief was based on a learner's age and Jo's on a learner's behaviour. There are many other bases for beliefs about learners, for example their ethnic or cultural background, social background, gender, disability, personality and so on. Reflecting on the beliefs you hold and the assumptions you make about your learners requires honesty and a willingness to ask yourself some personal *why* questions. And this can be challenging. Yet it can be a catalyst for improving your practice and helping you to better promote diversity and inclusion.

Critical thinking activity

Consider a group of your learners and reflect on the following questions.

» *Can you identify beliefs you have about any of them?*

» *Are your beliefs about them legitimate?*

» *Have they informed your teaching and if so how?*

» *What can you learn from this for the future?*

Values

As a teacher you are bound by your professional values. They are visible, shared with your colleagues and they help to give you your professional identity and guide you in your professional practice. They are also written down, included in the Education and Training Foundation (ETF) Professional Standards (Appendix 3). In addition to professional values, you will have your own personal values that you have developed from your cultural values. Cultural values are those we gain from belonging to certain groups: family, peer group, local and even national groups. Our personal values guide and inform our actions both personally and professionally.

The expectation is that your personal values are pretty much the same as your professional values but there is a fly in the ointment here. Personal values differ from professional values in one important respect; they are implicit and therefore often unacknowledged, so their influence on your practice may not necessarily be known to you. This state of affairs is summed up neatly by the contemporary British philosopher Mary Midgley who talks about our values as part of the

… metaphorical concepts or myths we live by … They are the matrix of thought, the background that shapes our mental habits. They decide what we think important and what we ignore. This is why we need to watch them so carefully.

(Midgley, 2004, p 4)

Bringing personal values into the open and examining them through the reflective process is one valuable way of developing your teaching. This process of 'watching values carefully' and gaining awareness of their influence is illustrated in the following two case studies.

CASE STUDIES

Lin's values

Lin has recently moved to England from Beijing where she used to teach English to Chinese learners. She is now teaching Mandarin Chinese in an FE college. This is an extract from her learning journal in which she reflects on her first month's experience in her new job and which she will discuss with her mentor who has been appointed to support her in her first year of employment.

This has been a real culture shock for me. In China I was used to just telling the students what to do and being confident they would do it. Basically they didn't argue and took it for granted that I was the expert who knew best. When I started here I assumed my new students would be the same, but they definitely weren't! They kept interrupting when I was explaining things, often challenging what I was saying and a couple of them were really disruptive. After one or two lessons their behaviour was getting worse, only a few seemed motivated to work hard and it wasn't an enjoyable experience either for them or for me.

My mentor suggested that I could try and give them more of a say in how we went about things rather than just expecting them to accept my way of doing things. This seemed alien to me and I felt uncomfortable with it. But since my conversation with my mentor I have tried to follow her suggestions and things have been easier. I've realised that my ideas about the role of a teacher that are OK in China won't work here. These students aren't prepared to sit back and do what the teacher tells them the whole time, and they are much more prepared to challenge and question me in a way that my students in Beijing would never do. I'm now beginning to develop ways to change my approach to teaching that helps the students rather than having a constant battle with them.

Paul's values

Paul teaches on a community learning course and is working towards a teaching qualification. A number of Paul's learners are not as enthusiastic as they appeared to be at the start of the term. He has asked an experienced colleague if he can help and he records what happened in his reflective journal.

When I explained the problem to Kerem he asked me to describe a typical session and then suggested it might help if I give them more opportunities for discovering things for themselves; individual research, group work and so on, and see what happened. I said I would give it a go and let him know how well it worked but privately the idea didn't grab me and I was reluctant to try it. I didn't see why it should make any difference – either they were interested or they weren't, so I didn't immediately make any changes. Things didn't improve over the next couple of sessions so in the end I suppose I was more or less forced to give it a go.

I think my learners were a bit surprised by the changes but set about their tasks with more enthusiasm than I'd seen since the beginning of term so I was left with egg on my face. Then something happened which stopped me in my tracks. At the end of the session I asked the class what they thought about the changes and they all agreed they'd really enjoyed the class. But as they began to wander off for lunch, Harry, one of the more vocal of my learners shouted out 'What took you so long?'.

Harry's accusation was a critical moment for me because I just didn't have an answer. I didn't know why I'd been so reluctant to let them take more control of their learning and so I was forced to reflect on reasons for this decision. Why did I always want to be the one at the front passing on my knowledge to receptive ears? This sort of personal reflection wasn't easy but I stuck at it and I learned:

- I get a kick out of being looked up to and passing on my expertise to others;

- I am good at expressing knowledge clearly and fluently;

- I assumed that my way was the best way.

In many ways making the changes to my teaching style that Kerem recommended was the easy bit – the problem has been solved. But realising how much I value being the 'know it all' is harder and it is going to be a challenge exploring how this might affect other aspects of my teaching and my relationships with my learners and my colleagues.

Lin's reflective experience was initiated by a problem that was getting worse and needed to be solved. Suggestions from her mentor improved the situation and led Lin to identify and then to modify the cultural values that had, up until then, been guiding her professional practice.

Paul's reflective experience was more complex. It was initiated by a throwaway comment from one of his learners that forced him to search for an answer. Paul had an uncomfortable reflective journey but it led him to recognise and then to begin to challenge some of the values that had informed his approach to teaching. This insight helped him to develop and improve his teaching.

There is one final point to bring out from Paul's experience: his personal values are unlikely to be identical to those of his learners and colleagues. You too will interact with people with very different values from yours. You might, for example, value punctuality where some of your learners do not or you might value plain speaking and some of your colleagues do not. So there is real potential here for clashes of values. Reflecting on the values you hold and how they might inform your approach to your learners and your colleagues will help you to identify any potential clashes, thus minimising the likelihood of conflict and increasing the chances of building positive relationships.

Critical thinking activity

»   *Consider your approach to your practice. In what ways would you say it is informed by your personal values?*

Reflection: single and double loop learning

The experience of reflecting critically involves two levels of learning and both levels are illustrated in the four case studies you have just been reading. Chris Argyris and Donald Schön (1974) called the first level of learning single loop learning. For example, Paul changed his style of teaching so that his learners were more in control of their learning and this tactic solved the problem of their lack of enthusiasm. This represents the type of reflection that occurs when you do something that does not work, then reflect on the issue and then try something else.

Argyris and Schön also identified a more sophisticated level of reflection that they defined as double loop learning. This occurs when you go further and begin to focus on and question the values, beliefs and assumptions that guide your actions. When Paul began to reflect on why he was initially reluctant to make changes to his teaching style he was questioning some of the values and assumptions that had guided his actions: this is an example of double loop learning.

Critical thinking activity

»   *Research single and double loop learning online, focusing on the work of Chris Argyris and Donald Schön.*

»   *Look again at the other three case studies 'Gillie', 'Jo' and 'Lin'. Identify examples of both single loop and double loop learning.*

»   *Reflect on a recent problem in your teaching. How did you decide what to do to solve the problem? Would you describe your learning from the experience as single or double loop learning?*

Conclusion

The process of reflecting on yourself requires an open mind and honesty and the experience can sometimes be uncomfortable. However, there are the rewards of improved practice through increased confidence, flexibility, creativity and control over what you do and say.

> *Through each experience we may gain new understandings and skills and our beliefs about ourselves, others and the world are challenged, changed or reinforced.*
>
> (Boud et al, 1985, p 69)

The aim of this chapter has been for you to recognise through the reflective process the relationship between you as an individual and your teaching. The focus has been on how your personality or character, your self-perception, your beliefs and your values inform your actions. In the following chapter, these themes will be developed and applied to communicating with your learners and colleagues and to managing behaviour.

Chapter reflections

» *Reflecting on your personality will help you to identify how it influences your approach to teaching and your learners.*

» *Reflecting on your strengths can help you to create an image of best practice; reflecting on your successes can help you to develop your talents and skills and increase your confidence and self-esteem.*

» *Reflecting on your self-perception can provide you with a more honest and balanced assessment of your practice.*

» *Reflecting on your beliefs and values can help you to learn how they inform your teaching; recognising and challenging them requires honesty and an open mind.*

» *Changing your actions following reflecting to solve a problem can be described as single loop learning; double loop learning questions the values, beliefs and assumptions that guide your actions.*

Taking it further

Stott, N (2010) How Previous Experience Can Shape Our Teaching, in Wallace, S (ed) *The Lifelong Learning Sector Reflective Reader.* Exeter: Learning Matters.

Neil Stott explains how his initial teaching style arose from his own previous experience of education, and puts forward some suggestions on how to extend your range and move out of your comfort zone.

Lawrence, D (2000) *Building Self-Esteem with Adult Learners*. London: Paul Chapman Publishing.

Although primarily focusing on enhancing learners' self-esteem, this book has some relevant sections on self-awareness and on developing your personal and professional skills.

References

Argyris, C and Schön, D (1974) *Theory in Practice: Increasing Professional Effectiveness*. San Francisco: Jossey-Bass.

Boud, D, Keogh, R and Walker, D (1985) *Reflection: Turning Experience into Learning*. London: Kogan Page.

Fook, J and Gardner, F (2007) *Practising Critical Reflection: A Resource Handbook*. Maidenhead: OU Press.

Ghaye, T (2010) *Teaching and Learning Through Reflective Practice*. London: Routledge.

Kennett, K (2010) Professionalism and Reflective Practice, in Wallace, S (ed) *The Lifelong Learning Sector Reflective Reader*. Exeter: Learning Matters.

Midgley, M (2004) *The Myths We Live By*. Abingdon: Routledge.

Peterson, C and Seligman, M (2004) *Character Strengths and Virtues*. Washington DC: American Psychology Association and Oxford University Press.

Rogers, J (2001) *Adults Learning*. Buckingham: OU Press.

Zwozdiak-Myers, P (2012) *The Teacher's Reflective Practice Handbook*. London: Routledge.

5 Reflective practice: communicating and managing behaviour

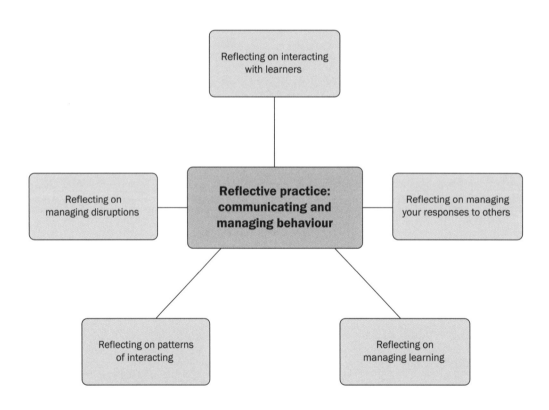

Chapter aims

This chapter will help you to:

*   reflect on ways to develop your teaching through effective communication;

*   reflect on and manage your responses to others;

*   reflect on ways to interact with learners to support their learning and to manage disruptions;

*   recognise the difference between espoused theory and theory in use.

Introduction

In the previous chapter you saw how reflective practice can help you to learn how your personality, self-perception, beliefs and values inform your actions and your teaching. This chapter continues that theme via a number of case studies focusing on communicating with learners and colleagues. It opens with reflecting on interacting with learners. It then explores reflecting on managing responses to others, identifying patterns of interacting, interacting to engage and motivate learners and to manage disruptions.

Reflecting on interacting with learners

Whether you are a new teacher or an experienced one, time spent reflecting on how you interact with your learners can provide you with valuable insights on possible opportunities to develop your communications skills. The following case study illustrates how one teacher set about doing this.

CASE STUDY

Evelyn's interactions

Evelyn is an experienced healthcare specialist who has just joined the training department within her healthcare organisation. She is working towards a teaching qualification and is recording in her reflective journal some concerns she has about how she interacts with her learners.

I was so pleased when I got this training job, as I am keen to pass on my skills and knowledge to others. The problem is I don't seem to be very good at it. It's not that I don't know what I'm talking about – I do, inside out. It's just that I don't seem to be very good at getting it across and it's starting to affect my confidence. It's not just nerves – I know it sounds stupid but it's as much that I don't know how to be with the trainees, how to talk to them and I think they sense it, which doesn't help.

My employer has assigned me a mentor, Justine, and the first thing she did was to invite me to sit in on one of her training sessions and now that I have watched her teaching I can see that it is very different from the sessions I've done so far. I noticed immediately that the atmosphere in her class was relaxed, everyone working and helping each other, and there was also a real buzz – Justine seems to know how to relate to them. My classes seem dull and stilted in comparison.

My initial reaction to observing Justine's class was to wish I hadn't – it really knocked my confidence and I confided as much to her in the feedback session. She tried to put my mind at ease about it, said I shouldn't worry, lots of new teachers feel like this and I would become more relaxed and confident as I gained experience. She did suggest I re-read the section on communication in one of my course books. So I took her advice and it was all there, making eye contact, speaking clearly, smiling and so on – I'd just not taken it all in properly when I'd read it first time round.

I decided to try and keep some of these tips in my head and when I had the next session with my group I made myself stand up straight and look around and smile. I think they were a little surprised but it felt OK because I actually got one or two smiles back – I didn't expect that – and I think it was more relaxed after that. So I am going to continue with my plan and try to include everything on my list.

There is one thing that I am beginning to learn and I think it is important. I've been so tied up with what I'm doing, being on show, trying to get it right that I've not thought enough about my trainees and I am beginning to see that it should be the other way round. Communication isn't just about me. It's as much about the trainees, thinking about them, being interested in them. Justine has brought this home to me – she interacted with her trainees like she really enjoyed their company – she listened to them and gave them her attention. There was something in that communication book I read about modelling – it's about copying the actions and behaviour you admire in someone. Perhaps I could model myself on Justine. I think I'll ask her if I can observe another of her teaching sessions.

Evelyn was concerned about how she came across to her learners, something probably experienced by a majority of new teachers. Facing a group of learners for the first time can be daunting and it can be quite a challenge working out the best way forward. Reflecting on how you interact with your learners can help you to manage this challenge and offers possibilities for you to develop and enhance your practice.

Critical thinking activity

Reflect on how you communicate with your learners. You might find the following questions helpful.

» *How confident and relaxed do you feel?*

» *What do you find easy?*

» *What do you find difficult?*

» *What help is available within your organisation to support you in developing your communication skills?*

This chapter opened with an illustration of a teacher working through a process of reflection to find ways to develop her communication skills and improve her interaction with her learners. Yet Evelyn's experience was far from typical. To begin with she was lucky enough to work within a supportive organisation, one that provided help in the form of a mentor. She also seemed to have receptive and accommodating learners, and from her journal entry there is no evidence of other pressures. Clearly, this is not the arena that many teachers have to operate in, which in reality is often characterised by huge workloads, time pressures, difficult and demanding learners and harassed colleagues. Negotiating your way around this more typical scenario is not easy but the task is more manageable if you are able to reflect on how you as an individual respond to and interact with those around you. How might this be achieved?

Reflecting on managing your responses to others

Our responses to others always have an emotional element. For example, even the simple response of listening attentively to a learner or colleague will, through eye contact, convey your interest and enthusiasm. Positive emotions such as interest, enjoyment, humour and so on are vital in teaching; they help us to engage, motivate, encourage and support learners. But situations can arise where it is all too easy to respond with irritation, anxiety or frustration. These negative emotions are disruptive; they act as a barrier to communication and are never helpful in finding solutions or in promoting and sustaining professional relationships. Reflecting on how you respond to learners and colleagues can help you to identify and then to manage disruptive emotions. The following case study illustrates the reflective process involved.

CASE STUDY

Aamir's responses

Aamir is an ICT specialist who works for a consultancy that provides training for the employees of local businesses. He has had a difficult few days and shares his problems with Lisa, a good friend and former colleague, over a coffee at the end of the week.

'I've had a rotten week and I'm fed up. Two of the guys in this latest group I've got, Tony and Alan, are a real pain in the neck. My new co-trainer Terry is getting on my nerves, and to crown it all, the manager at this place is doing his best to make life difficult for me.'

Lisa is sympathetic to Aamir's problems but she reminds him that he takes everything personally and sometimes responds without thinking. The best thing he can do, she suggests, is to reflect on what happened with each of these difficult people and try and look at each event objectively. With a parting comment to Lisa that she must have eaten a psychology book for her lunch, Aamir goes home to wind down and reflect on her suggestion. He knows that he wants to develop as a teacher and, if he does nothing, things are just going to carry on as they are; so he decides to have a go at taking Lisa's advice. He begins by writing down the events of the past few days as objectively as he can. This is Aamir's record of what happened.

Tony and Alan are a pair of 'know-it-alls' and they don't miss an opportunity to make me look small. They're on home ground – I'm the outsider and they let me know it. They're both a fair bit older than me, came up through the ranks so to speak, got their hands dirty en route. The latest dig came yesterday when I had to correct Tony after he made a calculation error. He told me he reckoned I'd been mollycoddled, that daddy must have paid for my degree. He made me feel like a kid and I started defending myself, blurting out that I'd put myself through university working in the local chippie at every chance I got. He knew he'd got to me and the chances are that from now on he'll probably take every opportunity to have a dig at me. I can see this wasn't the right way to handle the situation and I need to work out a better response.

Terry my co-trainer just makes me angry. At the team meeting last week he was all sweetness and light telling Rob our line manager how keen he was to pull out all the stops and do a good job. Once away from Rob's radar he's lazy and careless. So when he turned up yesterday without the handouts that I'd asked him to do, I just lost it, told him to pull his finger out or I'd be having a word with Rob. I vented the full force of my irritation on him, but now I've got to think about how we are going to manage to work together in future.

As for the manager at this place, he's gone out of his way to obstruct me from day one. What really annoyed me most though was when he changed the training room on Wednesday without even letting me know. I arrived to find a notice on the locked training room door to say that we'd been moved to B7, a pokey, dismal room on the top floor with no smart board or projector. I was so irritated I went straight to his office to have it out with him. I did get quite heated but he wouldn't budge, just sat there, saying he needed the room for his planning meeting later. In the end I just walked out – not the best response because I'm going to have to negotiate with him in future.

Having written everything down, Aamir read over what he'd written and he saw that Lisa was right – it was there in black and white on the page in front of him. He didn't stop and think; he just blundered on and then felt bad afterwards – resentful and stupid. Aamir knew that he didn't want to continue in this way. He had to try and respond to problems calmly and rationally rather than emotionally. He decided to start there and then by reflecting on some of the things Tony and Alan had said in the past and then practising responding calmly and confidently to their comments. He knew it would be harder when he had to do it for real but discovered that going through the process actually made him feel more confident.

A few weeks later Aamir and Lisa went out for a meal together. He could not wait to tell her that things had started to look up. No change on the manager front yet he told her, but he had been working on responding to Tony and Alan with a friendly smile and a change of topic and it seemed to be doing the trick – neither of them had made a dig at him since and the best thing was it actually made him feel better and more confident. Lisa congratulated him and asked how things were going with Terry. '*That's work in progress*' he told her, '*Last week I caught myself right in the middle of having a go at him*'. '*Good,*' she replied, '*that's a great start but next time catch yourself before you have a go at him! And don't forget that thinking before you act means no complaining, no sarcastic comments or put-downs. And watch the body language: no shrugs, no long sighs and definitely no eyes to heaven!*'

Critical thinking activity

» *Compare the nature of Aamir's initial reflections (his coffee break chat with Lisa) with his subsequent written reflections. To what extent do they illustrate a process of effective reflective practice as described in Chapter 2?*

» *Reflect on how you talk to your learners, to your colleagues and to others. What do your words and the way you use your voice tell them? What does your body language tell them? You might find it helpful to pair up with a colleague or friend you trust to give you some honest feedback.*

Reflecting on managing learning

Reflecting honestly and objectively on how you respond to those around you, as Aamir did, will give you insights on how you can enhance your relationships with learners and colleagues. Sometimes though, a situation may require you to be more inventive and creative and reflecting can help you to do this. The following case study shows how this might happen.

CASE STUDY

Lucas's intuition

Lucas is a newly qualified teacher who is finding it difficult to motivate some of his young learners on the Diploma in Public Service programme he teaches. In the following extracts from his journal he reflects on his problem.

Extract one

I've got this new group and some of them are causing me grief. Their enthusiasm levels are zilch. They mess about and don't pay attention. Then they don't have a clue what to do. I've tried to get them interested but nothing seems to work and I'm beginning to get fed up because their attitude is affecting the others in the class. I need to sort it out and fast. Why aren't they motivated? Is there something I'm not doing that could explain their lack of interest? I looked up 'Motivating learners' in one of my course books and it seemed I was already doing all the right things.

- *I'm enthusiastic about them and the programme.*

- *I'm friendly, I don't bite and I really care about how they do.*

- *I explain everything carefully and make sure they understand.*

- *I include everyone and try to get them all to join in.*

- *I try and get them to give their opinions and I listen to what they say.*

- *I try and get them to share their ideas and to work together.*

Critical thinking activity

» What suggestions could you offer Lucas to help him reflect on how he might motivate his recalcitrant learners?

CASE STUDY

Lucas's intuition

Extract two

Mulling over my problem I began to wonder whether perhaps I was looking at it the wrong way. Perhaps it wasn't a case of a problem with them or with me but more that I just needed to find the right tool to get them interested. And then I had a brainwave. It was a bit risky but it might just help – just a gut feeling. I hadn't read anything in my ITT course books about this but it seemed a good idea to me. Anyway, the idea came when I remembered Jake saying once that when he was a kid he really enjoyed doing magical tricks for his family, and it got me thinking about the idea of performing. So I had this idea of giving all my learners who want to, a chance to be the teacher, starting with Jake. I'm not sure how brave I feel about doing it but I think there are lots of them who would enjoy it and as long as I plan it really carefully, I think it might be a way forward.

Critical thinking activity

» What can you learn from these extracts about the effectiveness of Lucas's reflections?

In searching for reasons on why some of his learners were difficult to motivate, Lucas initially blamed himself; however, instead of leaving it there, he set out to examine the problem objectively. He then turned to literature to search for new ideas to motivate some of his learners but found nothing over and above what he was already doing. Thrown back on his own resources, Lucas began to look for a more creative solution. Sometimes theory is found wanting either because, as Lucas discovered, it is insufficient or because it does not work in practice. Theory does not necessarily always provide the answers you are looking for and then you find yourself thrown back on your own resources. This state of affairs can be uncomfortable; you are living with uncertainty about how to proceed, but on the other hand it can be a catalyst for you to be creative, to use your experience, your knowledge of your learners and even your intuition, as Lucas did, to find solutions.

Critical thinking activity

» *Can you think of an occasion when theory did not work for you in practice? Did you turn to your own wisdom and experience? What happened?*

Reflecting on patterns of interacting

The reflective process offers an opportunity for you to examine your own approach to communicating with your learners, to question your choices and decisions, to identify unconscious patterns in your communication style and to explore new approaches. You can observe this process in action in the following case study.

CASE STUDY

Lori's pattern of interaction

Lori teaches a group of adult learners on an Access to Higher Education programme at her local FE College. In the following extract from her journal she reflects on her approach to her teaching.

I am in the process of changing the way I approach my teaching, particularly how I interact with my learners. I started reflecting on this following one of the informal group meetings we have as part of CPD. We'd been talking about lesson planning and how important it was to create a variety of opportunities for our learners to be active and involved in making decisions and evaluating their learning. It's something we all strongly support and I said as much in the meeting. But even as I said it I was aware that there was a gap between what I'd said and what was actually happening in my practice. I don't think I'd realised it until then and I didn't like it.

So I decided to reflect on the gap between what I'd said and what I actually did, to work out what to do about it and to try and understand why it was there. Working out what to do was pretty straightforward. Basically, I spend too much time standing in front of my learners and talking to them and they spend too little time talking to me and each other. I have begun to explore ways to redress this imbalance.

Trying to understand the why has been more complex and it's also been uncomfortable. Straight away I latched on to the practical reason. We do work under enormous time pressure – there is an exam to take at the end and everything needs to be covered in time. But I think I've probably taken this path because it was the safest and most convenient option. I gave them the correct information. We went through it together and I backed it up with a handout. If I was being honest with myself, most of the time I was taking the easy way out. Then I just got into the habit of doing it that way and didn't question it.

An incident at a team meeting initiated a process of reflection for Lori: she said that she believed in learner-led learning but realised her own teaching style did not reflect this, something she had been completely unaware of. Reflecting on what she was actually doing in practice enabled her to see that it was her need to pursue the easiest option that habitually informed her teaching approach, rather than what she said she believed in.

Critical thinking activity

Reflect on how you interact with your learners. You might find the following questions helpful.

» *How do you decide which way to approach or to present a particular topic?*

» *What factors are involved in your choice?*

» *To what extent is your choice the best one for your learners?*

A need to keep to time constraints and a need for a safe and convenient option are two of the factors that influenced Lori's approach to her teaching. You might say these two needs were part of an unconscious model or map that guided her actions. This approach became a habit, so much so that Lori did not notice her learners' lack of involvement in their learning.

Mental maps

Each of us has our own view of the world around us: you could call it a mental map or model that guides our actions. Our beliefs, our values and the situation or context in which we operate play a significant role in the composition of our maps. Jeanne Hitching suggests that these maps or models

> *... act as a filter helping us to interpret events and manage our lives without becoming overwhelmed. ... (They) affect the way we think and strongly influence our behaviour.*
>
> (Hitching, 2008, p 19)

Our maps can lead us to think in certain ways without asking questions or considering alternatives. Mary Midgley suggests that our map:

> *... determines what we think important, what we select for our attention among the welter of facts that constantly flood in upon us.*
>
> (Midgley, 2004, p 2)

Like Lori, we are creatures of habit. It is easy to get into a set way of doing things where your mind goes into unthinking, automatic mode, much like the experience of driving from A to B and remembering none of the journey. For example, you may well be in automatic mode when you walk into a classroom or workshop and you greet your learners in the same way, go through the same physical actions, putting your bag or books down, standing or sitting in the same place and beginning the session in the same way. So the lesson here is to be alert to what is happening around you, to what your learners may be experiencing or feeling.

Engaging in reflective practice encourages you to become more aware of your mental maps. It compels you to look anew at what is actually happening in your teaching, especially at the small and subtle aspects, at what your learners are doing and what you are doing. It forces you to reassess your habitual practices. It requires you to question why you have chosen to do something in a certain way and it aids you in discovering the reasons for your choices and decisions.

Critical thinking activity

» *Can you identify and describe a mental map? How does it inform what you do?*

Espoused theory and theory in use

You may have come across the terms *espoused theory* and *theory in use* (Argyris and Schön, 1974). Both theories are illustrated in the two case studies you have just looked at and it is worth taking a closer look at what these two theories mean and the difference between them.

Espoused theory refers to theory that is *stated.* It encompasses:

*   theory that you find in print: books, articles, the internet and so on; Lucas, for example, turned to espoused theory when he researched how to motivate his learners;

*   theory that is stated when people say what they do; Lori for instance said that she was committed to learner-led learning.

Theory in use refers to what you do in practice. Lucas, for example, planned to motivate his learners by giving them a chance to be the teacher. Assuming he went ahead with his plan and his learners did take up the opportunity, this would become his theory in use.

There can sometimes be a gap between espoused theory and theory in use. For Lucas it was a case of the espoused theory on motivating learners not being adequate for his needs. Reflecting enabled him to create a workable theory, based on his knowledge of them and on his own intuition, that he could put into practice to motivate his recalcitrant learners.

Lori's experience was different. Her espoused theory, what she stated at the meeting, was that she valued learner-led learning. Yet her theory in use did not bear this out. In practice she spent a considerable amount of time talking to her learners. Her words were different from her actions. By reflecting on the gap between her espoused theory and her theory in use, Lori was able to make changes to her theory in use to bring it more in line with her espoused theory.

Lori is not alone in saying one thing and doing another. While we may articulate or espouse certain ideas about what we think and what we do, in practice it is implicit, unspoken theories in use that govern actions. The reflective process provides a framework that can be helpful in two ways. The first is in identifying your implicit theories in use to find out if and how they differ from your espoused theories. The second is when espoused theory, in the form of accepted theory, does not work out in practice; for example, when literature fails to provide you with answers. As Lucas discovered, this can be a spur to creating ideas using your intuition, knowledge, experience and wisdom to find solutions.

Critical thinking activity

» *Use the internet to research* espoused theory *and* theory in use *focusing on the work of Chris Argyris and Donald Schön.*

» *Reflect on one of your own espoused theories. Is there a gap between it and your theory in use? How might you bring them more in line?*

Reflecting on managing disruptions

Earlier case studies in this chapter have shown how, through the reflective process, communication can be used to manage learning and motivate learners. One important aspect of effective communication is the ability to recognise other people's viewpoints and feelings; the ability to empathise. Put another way, you could say that empathy is an understanding of other people's mental maps. How the reflective process can enable this understanding to develop can be seen in the following case study.

CASE STUDY

Erin: reflecting on her learners

Erin is a functional skills teacher at a small Agricultural and Equine College. She has taken over a group of learners on the Level 2 Diploma in Horse Care programme in place of Clare who is on sick leave. Erin records in her reflective journal her experience of the first session teaching her new group.

Extract one

My new group of learners are a real challenge and I'm feeling a bit stressed about how badly the first session went. For the first ten minutes I was the only one in the room, twiddling my thumbs and wondering whether I should go looking for them. Then two of them ambled in – another ten minutes before the rest turned up. It seems they went into town in the lunch break and forgot the time!

The bad start only got worse. They took ages to settle. Then within minutes, Courtney got up from her seat next to Jess and said 'I'm not sitting with her' and went to sit as far away as possible – apparently they'd been arguing all morning and this was just another round. I'd just managed to get them back working in groups when Brittany's phone rang. When I told her to turn it off she said 'Why do I have to? Clare lets us leave our phones on'.

Another ten minutes getting them all back on task, then when I went over to see how Amber's group was getting on I found the three of them pouring over a copy of Shout. *When I told them to put it away and get on with what they were supposed to be doing, they all pulled a face and Amber said, 'Do we have to, this class is so boring'. It looks like I'm stuck with this group for weeks or even months until Clare comes back so I'm going to have to get through to them somehow, otherwise they're not going to learn anything, to say nothing of the stressful time I'll have.*

Thinking about what happened objectively, I think one of the things that's very clear now is that I didn't deal with it all that well at the time – I didn't think on my feet – I just reacted, although one thing I am pleased about is that I was on the ball enough not to let my irritation show – and I was very irritated. So that was good but I need to work out why the session was wobbly in the first place so that I'm prepared for next time.

Critical thinking activity

»   *How might Erin use a reflective process to work out why the session was wobbly?*

Erin was already utilising perhaps the most useful tool at her disposal: staying calm. She now needs to identify potential opportunities to steer the class in a more productive direction. She continues to reflect, this time questioning her responses to her learners and trying to identify alternative strategies she can use.

CASE STUDY

Erin: reflecting on her learners

Extract two

OK so we got off on the wrong foot right from the start when they all came in late – I remember asking why they were late and reminding them they should have been there on time. Was that enough? Perhaps I could have been clearer about expecting them to come on time for the next session? I think first thing next session I will talk to them about what I expect from them and not just about time keeping.

The other thing I keep thinking about is Amber saying the class is so boring. Perhaps I could have asked her why and what would make it more interesting. And now that I've had a chance to think about it, I might even have been able to find a way to make use of that magazine they were reading. Perhaps I can do that next time. I'm certainly going to start the session with a class discussion about what I want from them and what they would like from me, to see if we can come to some sort of agreement.

Critical thinking activity

»   *Comment on the effectiveness of Erin's reflections above.*

Following the next session with her challenging learners, Erin continues with her journal.

CASE STUDY

Erin: reflecting on her learners

Extract three

Well, they all came in dribs and drabs again although not as bad as last week and once they were all there I told them that I wanted to make a contract with them and we needed to talk about what form it should take. This seemed to get their attention, they actually listened, we had quite a productive discussion and we managed to get a pretty fair consensus. But perhaps more importantly, I listened to them. It's been quite an eye-opener and now I am beginning to understand a bit of what Amber meant when she told me the classes were boring.

The thing is, it became very clear that most of them have come to college because they love horses and want to learn about them and how to look after them. It's horses that dominate their lives, and sitting in a classroom learning about writing and so on is way down on their list of priorities. Most of them see it as a necessary or unnecessary evil, depending on who you ask. I do see what they mean and so we have started to negotiate, to work on ways they can be more proactive and take more decisions on how we go about things, whilst ensuring that we cover what we need to. This isn't going to be easy to plan and manage but if this morning is anything to go by, I think we are going in the right direction.

Reflecting on what had happened in the first session with her new learners, on what they had done and what she had done, led Erin to plan how to work out a fresh approach. With this new approach that involved listening to what they had to say, she discovered that her learners had their own mental maps that guided their actions. In their mental maps time spent with horses was highly valued but time sitting in a classroom was not. Here was vital information on how they saw things, how they felt about being in a classroom, and it ultimately provided the reasons for their behaviour. These insights helped Erin to find ways to manage their behaviour and support their learning.

Every learner you meet will have his or her own mental map, which guides their actions and one way you can come to recognise these maps is through reflective practice. Recognising and accepting that learners have different values which in some cases may be vastly different to yours does not signal a requirement for you to relinquish what you see as worthwhile and important, and you will have noticed that Erin was not prepared to compromise with regard to what she felt her learners needed to do and achieve. Engaging in reflective practice can help you to find ways to take learners' maps into account, when planning how best to support them. As Marton et al (1997) suggest, *'it is a good idea to recognise your learners' views of their world and the effect this has on their approach to learning'*. You may well need to adjust your teaching accordingly.

Critical thinking activity

» *Reflect on a group of your learners. Can you identify, from what they do and say, the things that are important to them and/or how they feel? What can you learn from this to help you in future planning?*

Conclusion

Reflecting on communicating with learners can provide some important insights into your approach, your practice and your relationships with learners and colleagues. This should enable you to build positive and productive relationships, to enthuse and motivate your learners and to manage their learning and behaviour. These insights are also important in considering your own development as a teacher in FE. This is the subject of the next chapter.

Chapter reflections

» *Reflecting on how you interact with those around you can help you to develop ways to improve your teaching and build positive relationships.*

» *The reflective process provides a framework that can be helpful in identifying your mental maps and in reassessing your habitual practices; it can help you to be creative, to use your experience, your wisdom and your intuition in finding solutions.*

» *Reflecting can help you to support your learners by understanding their mental maps and being aware of their views and their feelings.*

» *Espoused theory is theory that is stated either in written form or stated verbally. Theory in use is what you do in practice; there can sometimes be a gap or mismatch between espoused theory and theory in use.*

Taking it further

Appleyard, N and Appleyard, K (2010) *Communicating with Learners*. Exeter: Learning Matters.

There is much in this book to help you develop your communications skills, with chapters on listening and speaking skills, communicating for inclusivity and managing behaviour through communication.

Rogers, J (2007) *Adults Learning.* Maidenhead: OU Press.

This accessible book is full of helpful, practical information on interacting with adult learners.

References

Argyris, C and Schön, D (1974) *Theory in Practice: Increasing Professional Effectiveness*. San Fransisco: Jossey-Bass.

Hitching, J (2008) *Maintaining Your Licence to Practice.* Exeter: Learning Matters.

Marton, F, Hounsell, D and Entwhistle, N (1997) *The Experience of Learning: Implications for Teaching and Studying in HE*. Edinburgh: Scottish Acadamic Press. Cited, Walters, D (2007) Who Do They Think They Are? Students' Perceptions of Themselves as Learners, in Campbell, A and Norton, L (eds) *Learning, Teaching and Assessing in Higher Education.* Exeter: Learning Matters.

Midgley, M (2004) *The Myths We Live By*. Abingdon: Routledge.

6 Reflective practice and continuing professional development

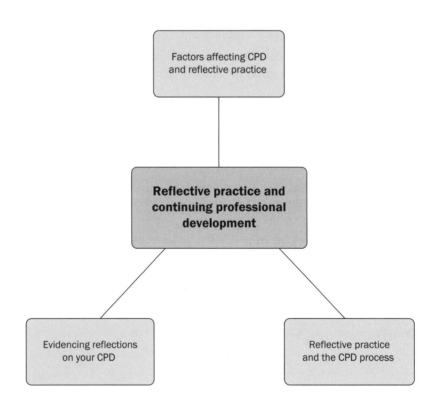

Factors affecting CPD and reflective practice

Reflective practice and continuing professional development

Evidencing reflections on your CPD

Reflective practice and the CPD process

Chapter aims

This chapter will help you to:

- understand how reflective practice contributes to effective CPD;

- apply reflective practice techniques to planning, undertaking and evaluating your own CPD.

Introduction

If you visit any professional for advice or to get a job done, be it doctor, accountant or electrician, you expect the service you receive to be of high quality, delivered with expertise and using up-to-date methods and equipment. After all, you would not be happy if your dentist was still using equipment and techniques that he/she used at dental school 25 years previously. The same criteria apply to teaching; it is incumbent on you to keep up to date and develop your professional skills in order to provide a professional service for your learners. In other words, you need to undertake CPD throughout your career.

This chapter looks at CPD from the viewpoint of reflective practice. It starts by identifying some important factors that affect CPD and influence the nature of your critical reflection. This is followed by an analysis of the CPD process and is illustrated by scenarios featuring teachers at different stages of their professional careers, reflecting in a variety of ways.

Factors affecting CPD and reflective practice

There are some significant features of CPD for FE teachers that will affect your reflective practice. You need to take into account:

- the nature of dual professionalism;

- the changing FE environment;

- your changing needs as you gain experience.

The nature of dual professionalism

Keeping up to date and developing professional skills is not always easy. One reason for this is that your role as a teacher in FE is a dual one, in the sense that you are acting as a professional teacher and a professional in your subject specialism at the same time. In addition to developing your teaching skills you also need to keep up to date in your specialist subject in order to retain your credibility with your learners and colleagues.

This issue is illustrated by the story of Ieva, a former social worker who is now a teacher in FE.

CASE STUDY

Ieva's dilemma

Ieva has been employed as a lecturer in social work for five years, during which time she has successfully qualified as a teacher. Previously, she worked as a social worker for ten years and feels that she is in danger of getting out of date in her specialist area. She raises this issue while chatting with her line manager over a cup of coffee.

The thing is that I've spent so much time over the past two years working on my Cert Ed that I feel I've lost touch with what it's like to be a social worker. There's been so much new regulation introduced, particularly to do with child welfare. Many of my old colleagues in the office have left and I really feel out of touch with the local social work scene. I can't see it getting easier because there seems to be an endless round of meetings, admin, new procedures and general hassle in college that takes up all my working day. My classes deserve better than to be taught by someone who knows little more about the current problems and stresses of social work than the learners we send out on work experience.

Critical thinking activity

»   *Consider how Ieva might keep up to date in her specialist subject while developing her expertise as a teacher and coping with a stressful job at the same time.*

The changing FE environment

Anyone who has worked in FE for more than a few years will attest to the fact that the job is vastly different today compared to the situation when they started. There are constant changes to the curriculum to reflect service users' needs, technological changes (particularly concerning ILT), new legislation and regulation, amendments to conditions of service, not to mention the inevitable local changes that come with college reorganisation or the closure of a major employer near your place of work. Here is James, reflecting on how his job as a teacher training tutor has altered over the past ten years.

CASE STUDY

James's recollections

When I started teaching, the college was just running the first year of the local university's Cert Ed course and a City and Guilds Introduction to Teaching course. Then the 2007 regulations were introduced and we decided to change to the new DTLLS and PTLLS courses with all the curriculum and admin work that entailed. Not only that, but the college decided to ensure that all staff would be teacher trained by 2010, and gain the licence to practise offered through the Institute for Learning. Then, of course, along comes the Lingfield report, and we revert to the voluntary system that we originally had before 2007!

While all this was going on we were involved in two major Ofsted inspections and a new Principal was appointed whose first job was to review the college structure and save half a million pounds. You can guess the result: fifteen staff made redundant and my section lost one lecturer when Harry retired and was not replaced.

It's still a great job; I really enjoy the teaching and get a kick out of seeing my group becoming better teachers. But it's tough and the pace of change doesn't look like slowing down in the next couple of years.

Critical thinking activity

» *James's reflections detail a series of developments that were out of his control – they were visited on him by outside agencies and he had to respond as best he could. Identify the major pressures and changes to your own job in the recent past and reflect on how this affects your CPD.*

Your changing needs as you gain experience

It is not only external pressures that affect your CPD. Equally important is how you see your career developing. There may be opportunities for promotion, either within your organisation or by applying for a new job elsewhere. Family circumstances may change, limiting or expanding the professional opportunities open to you. You may wish to develop your skills in new areas, or just have a change to keep you fresh and involved with your subject and your learners. In any event, it is your career and your aspirations that matter, and regular reflection on what you want to do in the future is a key tool in managing your CPD.

Even if you are entirely happy with the job you are doing, your professional development needs will change throughout your career, and your skills of reflection will develop as well. If you have recently qualified as a teacher you will have the benefit of recent knowledge and understanding gained during teacher training, but it is likely that you will have relatively little teaching experience. As you gain experience your profile changes. Stuart and Hugh Dreyfus (1980) described this development as *a progression from novice to expert.* The novice starts with a strict reliance on rules and progresses through advanced beginner, competence and proficiency stages to expert status where behaviour and performance become almost intuitive. Susan Wallace (2007) describes a similar model by Anthony Gregorc who envisaged a four-stage process that he called *becoming, growing, maturing and fully functional.*

> *The development needs he identifies for the first stage, Becoming – focusing on the use of methods and resources and the skills of planning – might be referred to as a survival kit for teachers. … In the next phase, Growing, the teacher's development needs are for consolidation and expansion of these skills and strategies. The third phase, which Gregorc labels Maturing, involves strong personal commitment, increased willingness to experiment and an ability to tolerate ambiguity … (In) the final Fully Functioning phase the teacher has developed a high level of self-direction and astute skills of self-evaluation based on self-referenced norms. Here*

the teacher's needs move definitively into the area of self-development and will lead the teacher to seek continuing opportunities for personal and professional growth.
(Wallace, 2007, p 76)

You can see from this analysis that as you gain experience you will also gain knowledge and understanding that cannot be obtained from reading books or undertaking courses. This is the knowledge that is captured by critical reflection on incidents and events that you experience in the course of your daily routine. It is unique to you and it is also valuable, as illustrated by Penny's story.

CASE STUDY

Penny's knowledge

Penny has been teaching for 15 years in a large FE college, and currently she is mentor to Jusuf, a probationary teacher in his first year of teaching. Jusuf has just observed Penny teach a BTEC class, and this is one of his comments to Penny about the experience.

You make it all look so easy and effortless and you seem to have a sixth sense on what approach to adopt when something crops up. For instance, during the group work a couple of the groups were making a bit too much noise and starting to distract the others. What I noticed was that you dealt with the groups differently. You just went over to the first group and whispered to them and they were quiet, but with the second group you asked Jason to come and have a word individually, and he worked on his own for ten minutes before re-joining his group and they finished the task quietly as well.

The thing is, I couldn't see what was different in each group's behaviour and I'd just have told all of them to work quietly, probably causing resentment and a lot of grumbling. How on earth do you know what tactics to adopt in these situations? I don't think I'll ever have that sort of sensitivity with my classes.

The key point of this story is that Penny's effective classroom management was based on unique knowledge gained from her 15 years of teaching. She realised that the first group were co-operating well and just needed to be calmed down a bit. However, in the second group she recognised that the problem was centred around one learner, Jason, who had a history of being hyper-active and was disrupting the group. By taking him out of the group for a while the other learners could get back to work, and Jason could complete his part of the task on his own before going back to the group. Jusuf did not have a level of experience to match this unique understanding, and it is not surprising that he felt a bit overwhelmed. The development needs of these two teachers are inevitably different, but the process of critical reflection that enables them both to identify their individual needs is essentially the same.

Similarly, reflecting on the nature of your CPD is likely to be affected by how far along the spectrum from novice to experienced teacher you are, and an objective and logical CPD process is valid for any stage of your career and gives ample opportunity for critical reflection.

Reflective practice and the CPD process

Depending on whether you are working in a large college, a small private training agency, an industrial training centre or any of the other myriad institutions that make up the diverse FE sector, there are going to be major differences in the way CPD is viewed, supported and managed. Some large organisations will have sophisticated appraisal systems that provide a framework for the professional development of all their staff; other smaller service providers will have neither the resources nor the capability to provide this level of support. To a large extent, professionals in these organisations will be responsible for their own CPD. However, in spite of such wide differences, there are some general features of CPD that are valid wherever you work. What is more, there is a wide range of resources available to help you, and a good starting point for this is the material produced by the Institute for Learning (IfL).

The IfL was established in 2002 to support FE teachers in gaining and maintaining a licence to practice and the institute constantly emphasised the importance of reflective practice in relation to CPD. Hitching (2008) describes the fundamental approach of the IfL.

> *You as practitioner are central to the process [of reflective practice] ... it is integral to the whole process of professional growth. It begins with ... examining your practice as a means to identifying your professional needs. It continues with you setting out these needs clearly as a set of measurable objectives and engaging in activities to achieve them.*
>
> (Hitching, 2008, p 13)

Although the IfL was disbanded in 2014, you may find that their model of the CPD process is relevant to your situation. These are the stages of the CPD process that the IfL identified:

* reflect on your practice to date;

* identify your development needs, expressed in terms of measurable objectives;

* identify the best development activities to meet these needs;

* carry out the development activity;

* reflect on the outcomes of the development activity;

* identify future development needs based on these outcomes.

You may notice the parallels between this model and the cyclical model of reflective practice introduced in Chapter 2 (reflection, action, more reflection, revised action, ad infinitum). The CPD cycle can be integrated with this reflective practice cycle in a single diagram, as shown in Figure 6.1.

This close link between CPD and reflective practice can be illustrated at all the stages of the CPD cycle, beginning with identifying your development needs by reflecting on your current practice.

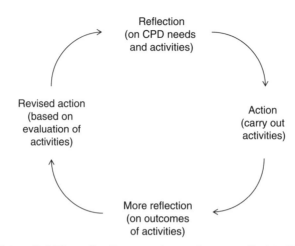

Figure 6.1 *The reflective practice cycle as applied to CPD.*

Reflecting on your practice to date and identifying development needs

Reflecting on your experience in order to identify your development needs is an approach that can be illustrated by the story of Arturo, who has been working as an FE teacher for just under one year, following a career in industry.

CASE STUDY

Arturo's self-appraisal

Arturo is due to have his first annual review. This is part of his college's quality assurance system and includes an interview with John, his line manager, to review his progress over the previous year and to plan for the coming year. The focus is on professional development in line with the college's five-year plan. Arturo's previous job was with a small engineering firm that did not have such a formal process, and he is apprehensive about the interview and how he should prepare for it. He asks for advice from Naomi who has been teaching in the college for the last eight years. This is what she says.

These interviews can actually be quite useful because if you know what you would like to do next year in terms of getting on in the college, this is a good opportunity to stake your claim. The most important thing is to be well prepared: write down what problems you've had and what you'd like to happen to solve them, tell John about the things you've really liked doing and anything new that you'd like to be involved in next year. I use a sort of SWOT analysis to sort my thoughts out, but it doesn't really matter how you prepare as long as you've done your homework.

Arturo knew all about SWOT analyses – identifying **s**trengths, **w**eaknesses, **o**pportunities and **t**hreats – because he had used this technique in his previous job to solve business problems. Therefore, he thought it was worth a try to prepare for his interview. He started by listing his strengths (good lesson preparation, good rapport with his learners) and weaknesses (getting trapped with individual learners, not keeping up with marking). Then he went on to identify opportunities (teaching the new level 3 course, volunteering to join the team going into schools to talk about his courses) and threats (pressure of admin, no funding for his PGCE course).

This was a good start – at least he had identified the good and bad points of his first year in the job, and started to think what he wanted to do next. He was then able to define his development needs. This is his list:

- time management, both in teaching and coping with admin;

- study for PGCE;

- gain experience in marketing my courses;

- gain teaching experience at level 3;

- improve classroom management skills.

Critical thinking activity

» *Review the key features of reflective practice described in Chapter 2. To what extent does Arturo's reflections on his work illustrate these features?*

One feature of being involved in an appraisal scheme like the quality assurance system at Arturo's college is that it is continuous. It provides the discipline of reviewing your CPD at regular intervals and thus embeds the cyclical and ongoing nature of good reflective practice. Additionally, the formal nature of the scheme ensures that your experience, aspirations and decisions are recorded.

As far as Arturo is concerned, the approach he adopted in using a SWOT analysis forced him to acknowledge his teaching problems in an objective fashion and with an open mind. You have already seen that this is not always easy to do; it seems a bit like dwelling on failure. But seen in the context of objective analysis of teaching as a skill in which nobody is perfect, it can now be presented as a non-threatening opportunity to improve with the chance of getting some support along the way. Another feature worth noting is that Arturo took advantage of his rapport with Naomi to gain advice, an example of using more than one source to reflect critically and constructively.

This process of critical self-appraisal is an essential first step in the CPD process and provides a good example of reflective practice in action. Arturo's list of development needs follows logically from his SWOT analysis and will form a good basis for his interview. There are, of course, many other ways of getting to this point, such as mapping your experience or just asking yourself a set of key questions. A typical list of such questions could include the following.

- What has gone well?

- What things have not gone so well?

- Why have they not gone so well?

- What needs to happen to improve these areas of difficulty?

- What support do I need?

- What changes in the way I work do I want to make in future?

The important things to remember are to be honest with yourself about your problems and to give equal consideration to both the good things and the difficulties you have experienced.

Critical thinking activity

»   *Reflect on the process you find most suitable to define your own development needs. Try using a SWOT analysis and the list of key questions above to determine which reflective approach to self-appraisal is most appropriate for you.*

Reflecting on activities to meet your development needs

Adopting a systematic reflective approach to meeting your development needs is as important as defining them. There are several ways of doing this. One of the most popular is to start by defining the outcomes you want from the activity. This is often referred to as defining *SMART* outcomes that meet the following criteria.

- **S**pecific   What exactly do you want to do?

- **M**easurable   How will you know when it is done?

- **A**ttainable   How can it be done?

- **R**elevant   How will it help me?

- **T**ime bound   When will it be completed?

Critical thinking activity

»   *Use this model to reflect on how your own development needs can best be met.*

You may feel that this approach, which is often used as part of a formal appraisal system, is somewhat mechanistic. However, it gives an idea of the type of information you need to back up your own feelings about what you want to do as part of your personal CPD programme and how you wish to set your priorities.

Even if you are not involved in a formal appraisal scheme, it is still possible to devise your own system for choosing development activities, tailored to your own specific needs. There is a whole range of activities that you can consider; formal courses, mentoring, observation of an experienced teacher, peer observation and action research to name but a few. Reflecting on the best choice will involve a variety of factors, which could include your own learning style, your relationship with colleagues, availability of resources, your previous experience and so on. This can again be illustrated by Arturo's story.

CASE STUDY

Arturo's CPD: development activities

Arturo has just finished his appraisal interview with John and is telling Naomi how it went.

I'm quite pleased really. I've got some of the things I wanted and can understand why the other things aren't possible yet, at least for the next year. It was a good discussion because John gave me the chance to talk about my time here in detail, and wasn't judgemental about what I thought he would see as failures, like not being able to keep up with my marking. It was more like he was on my side and it gave me confidence to be more open about problems. One thing was pretty clear – the time I'd spent on reflecting and writing down the successes and problems during the past year was really worthwhile. I was able to be confident about what I wanted from the interview and could back up my thoughts with examples.

One thing that I'd not considered enough was the problem John was facing in view of next year's budget cuts. In many ways his hands are tied and the bad news is that I won't be able to start my PGCE next year; the department just can't afford for me to be away for one day a week at the university, but John has promised to put my name forward for the course after twelve months. Also, there isn't much chance of me being timetabled for the new level 3 course because Mina and Peter have experience of teaching similar courses and both are keen to teach on this one.

On the other hand, John seemed very keen for me to be involved in the marketing work with schools, working with Ros as a sort of deputy. He even offered me a half hour remission from my teaching load and has arranged for me to go with Ros next week to St John's school so that I can see what she actually does.

We also had a discussion about my classroom problems: getting behind with admin and marking and not getting through lessons without being trapped by over-demanding learners. John offered to come and observe me to see if he could suggest any way of helping and also invited me to watch him teach the BTEC group, which is the one I seem to have most problems with. A couple of months ago I'd have been really apprehensive even talking to John about this, let alone him coming in to see me struggling with a difficult class, but it seems OK now because I think he wants to help rather than acting like some sort of inspector trying to find fault.

Finally, we spent a bit of time talking about how I saw my future in the college. He asked me what I'd like to be doing in five or ten years' time. I'd never really thought too much about this – I've been too busy getting through each day and it wasn't until we had that chat last week that I even gave a thought about next term, still less beyond next year. So we agreed to talk some more after he'd seen me teach.

Critical thinking activity

» *In what ways does Arturo's story illustrate how reflection can be used to identify appropriate professional development activities?*

As in the first extract of Arturo's story, this case study illustrates several features of reflective practice that come into play when you are planning your development activities.

Objective analysis of strengths and weaknesses

Arturo had the confidence to acknowledge his classroom management problems and see them not as a failure to be concealed but as a problem that could be solved by appropriate support. He was able to discuss his difficulties openly with John in spite of initial doubts ('*A couple of months ago I'd have been really apprehensive talking to John about this*'). Arturo's self-critical reflection paved the way to identifying a supportive and positive solution to the problem.

Consideration of a wide range of sources and methods

A second point to notice about Arturo's story is the wide range of development activities that you can consider when reflecting on the best way to achieve your CPD needs. Gone are the days when CPD seemed to be restricted to sending people on some form of training course. In addition to his proposed PGCE course, Arturo talks about observing an experienced teacher in action (John), having an experienced teacher observe one of his own lessons (John again) and shadowing a marketing professional to learn a new skill (Ros and schools liaison). Additionally, there are other possibilities you can consider when reflecting on potential choices of activity. Research projects, often involving action research (to be covered in detail in Chapter 9), study of theory, secondment to another organisation, developing a new course and taking on new responsibilities are all examples of such potentially effective development activities.

Being logical and realistic

This case study illustrates the need to take into account external factors when working out what activities you would like to pursue. Choice of activities needs to be set in the context not only of your own aspirations, but also of your work, the needs of your organisation and what realistic level of support might be possible. Naturally, if you can tailor your needs to fit the development priorities of your organisation, the better your chance of being successful in obtaining support. Arturo, a bit belatedly, realised this when he recognised that the college couldn't afford to send him on a PGCE course immediately, no matter how high this activity was on his list of development needs.

Consequently, in reflecting on what development activities to prioritise, it might be useful to design a prompt list that takes into account the opportunities and limitations of your work situation.

- What are the key tasks and responsibilities of your present post?

- What are the main implications of your organisation's development plans for your work?

- What skills do you have that could be used to greater advantage in line with your organisation's plans?

- How can you define your development needs in a way that will benefit your organisation as well as fulfilling your personal aspirations?

- What support and training activities are realistically available to you and your organisation that would meet your development needs?

Seeing reflective practice and CPD as continuous processes

You saw with the story of Penny and Jusuf earlier in this chapter how your professional development needs will change throughout your career. The same thing applies to your choice of CPD activities to meet these needs. Professional development isn't something that is completed at the end of a training course; it is a career-long process that changes and develops over your professional lifetime. In this sense it mirrors the key feature of reflective practice as being a continuous process.

In Arturo's narrative, John encourages him to take a long-term view by suggesting he should give some thought to his career aspirations ('He asked me what I'd like to be doing in five or ten years' time'). This will enable Arturo to prioritise his development needs as part of a long-term personal plan that can be reviewed regularly and amended as changing circumstances dictate. Regular reflection on your professional progress is the basis of making this review process as effective as possible.

The way in which different types of development activity often become more appropriate as your career progresses is illustrated by the following story of Arturo's line manager, John.

CASE STUDY

John's change of role

John is presently a senior lecturer who has been the curriculum leader for the computing section of the Business Studies department for eight years. He is now aged 52, having worked at the college for 15 years after a career as a computer programmer in industry. He has just accepted a transfer to a job in the professional development unit in the college, a cross-college post with responsibility for staff training and assuring the quality of teaching throughout the college.

After the initial euphoria of being selected for a new high-profile appointment, he is beginning to wonder what he has to let himself in for. After a chat with Raquel, his new line manager, he knows he is going to have many unfamiliar things to do. He will run the next ATL course, be a personal tutor to some learners on the DTL course, help in college preparations for the forthcoming Ofsted visit and give a presentation on the latest ILT developments as part of the next college training day. Here are the notes he makes as he reflects on what he needs to do in the six weeks before he takes up his appointment.

Things I need to do for starters:

Get up to date:

- Latest government initiatives that affect FE.
- Ofsted policies and procedures.
- College policies that affect staff training and teaching quality.
- Recent educational theory relevant to ITT courses.

Find out:

- Ofsted procedures and what happened at the last inspection.
- Details of current ATL and DTL programmes.
- College ILT plans.
- College training day details.

How to do it:

- Lots of research – internet and library for getting up to date.
- Talk to Syed who ran last college training day.
- Sit in on current ATL class – talk to staff and learners.
- Check evaluation reports on ATL and DTL courses.
- Visit Sally at Norbridge College (just finished Ofsted inspection of their ITT programme).
- Plan timetable of what I need to do before September and discuss with Raquel.

Critical thinking activity

»   *Compare John's reflections on his development needs and activities with Arturo's reflections in the previous case study. To what extent does the stage of John's career as an experienced and senior teacher lead to a different emphasis in his reflective practice as opposed to that of Arturo as a teacher relatively new to the profession?*

You have probably noticed that John has had the confidence and experience to identify a range of possibilities to prepare himself for his new role. These options include research into both practical and theoretical issues, observing other teachers and learners, visiting other organisations and discussing his plans with other experienced teachers. This is a slightly wider range of activities than that identified by Arturo, but the main difference in approach is that John was able to take full responsibility for identifying his own needs and to think of ways in which they might be met.

This demonstrates the reflective practice of a person who is at an advanced stage of the Dreyfus model mentioned earlier, where behaviour and performance become almost intuitive. Similarly it reflects Gregorc's fully functioning phase where '*the teacher has developed a high level of self-direction and astute skills of self-evaluation based on self-referenced norms ... leading the teacher to seek continuing opportunities for personal and professional growth.*' By contrast, Arturo is still relying on the advice of an experienced colleague in order to reach the most appropriate conclusions, akin to Dreyfus' *advanced beginner* stage and to Gregorc's *growing* stage.

Notwithstanding the career differences between these two teachers, both are using similar reflective processes to determine how best to meet their professional development needs. They are both reflecting on their experience and working out objectively what they need to do in future. Both are involved in an ongoing experience: being self-critical and open-minded, using a variety of sources and recording their reflections. In summary, they are both operating as reflective practitioners.

Using reflection to evaluate the outcomes of your development activity

Once you have embarked on a professional development activity, you need to continue to reflect on what you are doing and have some objective way of evaluating the outcomes; otherwise much of the benefit of undertaking the activity may be lost. This presupposes the existence of some structure to your reflection in order to ensure that you can collect evidence for your evaluation and capture the main learning points. In the previous case study John had this in mind when he made written notes to plan a timetable of preparations of the actions he intended to take; good evidence of structured and recorded reflection.

Using reflection as a tool to evaluate your CPD can be illustrated with Arturo's account of his observation of an experienced teacher at work.

CASE STUDY

Arturo's observation of an experienced teacher

Arturo has just observed John teaching a BTEC class. As John had to leave immediately afterwards to attend a meeting, he asked Arturo to write down an evaluation on how he felt the class had gone; good points, things that didn't go so well, what he would do differently and what he had learned. This is what Arturo wrote.

I really enjoyed watching this lesson, although I'm not sure I'll ever be able to teach as well as this. These were the good things I noticed:

1. *The way John dealt with Jason and Melanie who arrived ten minutes late. He didn't interrupt his briefing but just signalled to them to sit down and wait. When the rest started on their written task he spoke to them quietly and told them what to do. No disruption, apologies accepted. I had a similar incident last week when the late arrivals made a lot of fuss settling down which put me off my stroke and I had to repeat a lot of what I'd just been explaining.*

2. *The way John amended his plan when the group work overran. The learners were clearly involved and enjoying the task so postponing the following topic to the next class meant that their learning was not interrupted. I don't think I'd have had the confidence to do this; I'd have been worried about getting behind with covering the syllabus.*

3. *The way John dealt with Harriet who started to be a real pain in the group work. I think she doesn't like working with Loren, and she decided to keep on winding her up with snide comments. She was distracting everyone else in the group until John had a quiet word. I don't know what he said, but she was as good as gold afterwards. I must find out what he actually said. I think I'd have read her the riot act and probably caused even more disruption.*

There was a real buzz in this class that I wish I could replicate in mine. The students clearly respected John, were interested in the subject and were keen to learn. There doesn't seem to be as much life in a lot of the sessions I teach. They do the work but without the same commitment or enthusiasm. I don't really understand why – must talk to John and see if he has any tips.

Critical thinking activity

» *To what extent is this evaluation a critical reflection of Arturo's observation?*

You may think that this extract represents work in progress that will not be completed until John and Arturo have some face-to-face discussion on the observation. Arturo has identified incidents where he feels he can adopt John's approach to his own teaching. Being more flexible in adapting a lesson plan, dealing with latecomers and disruptive students are examples of this. This has given him some ideas to try out in his own practice but they are implicit. He states what he would normally have done (eg '*read Harriet the riot act*') and recognises the limitations of his present approach.

On the other hand, his evaluation is skewed in as much as he identifies strengths and does not mention any weaknesses or difficulties. Maybe this was an outstanding lesson that did not exhibit any problems, but it looks as though Arturo may have been concentrating exclusively on strengths. Nor has Arturo explicitly identified the main learning points, apart from implying that he may copy some of John's tactics, for example in dealing with latecomers. There is a slight sense of under-confidence: '*I'm not sure I'll ever be able to teach as well as this.*'

What is probably needed here is for Arturo to use a standardised observation pro forma to ensure all the key observation features were covered. He could then formulate a list of questions for John which will allow him to gain specific advice on those areas where he feels he needs help; for example, on how to create the *buzz in the class* that he observed. Once again, this scenario emphasises the point that reflective practice is a continuous process. Observation of an experienced teacher here is merely a starting point. It needs to be followed by a structured discussion between Arturo and John to determine an action plan of things for Arturo to practice in his own teaching, for him to put these ideas into practice and to evaluate how well they worked.

Evidencing reflections on your CPD

One point that has become clear from these CPD case studies is the importance of using evidence from a wide variety of sources as a key feature of reflective practice. This is particularly apposite when you are evaluating the effectiveness of the development activities you have undertaken.

Critical thinking activity

» *Look back at the development activities that Arturo and John planned, undertook and evaluated in the case studies in this chapter. In addition to their own point of view, what other sources were considered and used to inform their reflections on their CPD? Are there any other sources that they could have used? What are the potential benefits of using such sources?*

Arturo's reflections on his development needs were based primarily on his own perceptions which he used to analyse the problems he was experiencing and to identify the strengths he felt he brought to teaching. His use of a SWOT analysis showed a systematic approach that was both logical and objective. However, he also sought the advice of an experienced colleague, Naomi, and this use of other expertise was reinforced in the segment on development activities when John and Ros were suggested as mentors to advise and support him. This activity will generate observation reports and informal advice that will supplement Arturo's own evaluations and reflections.

There are also some other sources that Arturo could have considered to enrich his reflection. Firstly, there is feedback from his learners. This could include quantitative data (such as test results, absence records and retention rates) and qualitative information that would include evaluation sheets, informal chats with individual learners and learner reports used as part of the college's quality assurance scheme. Secondly, there is theoretical knowledge that Arturo can gain from the internet, journals and books on teaching skills and practice. Such theoretical knowledge often forms the backbone of ITT courses and distills a world of experience and expertise into a form that the fledgling teacher can use as an introductory guide to effective teaching. But this source is not restricted to novice teachers; it is equally valuable to experienced teachers to develop their teaching skills and to keep up to date with current developments.

This use of a variety of sources was well described by Stephen Brookfield (1995) with his theory of critical lenses. He argues that critically reflective teaching depends not just on your own perceptions but on information from at least three other sources. Consequently, for reflective practice to be truly critical it needs to be seen through four critical lenses:

1. your perceptions as a professional teacher;
2. the perceptions of your learners;
3. the perceptions of your colleagues;
4. educational theory.

Brookfield saw this as a process in which initially you form your own judgements. Then you test your conclusions by finding out your learners' opinions about your teaching, by using your colleagues as critical friends and justifying and evaluating your actions. Finally, you can check your conclusions against current theory. This approach can offer a comprehensive way of evaluating your development activities.

Conclusion

CPD is a key feature of teacher professionalism in which teachers are perennial learners, developing their professional skills throughout the whole of their career. Reflective practice and CPD are closely linked and the most effective CPD is planned, delivered and evaluated through critical reflective practice. It is possible to trace the features of reflective practice identified in this book through all stages of the CPD process and this is relevant to all FE teachers, no matter what stage of their professional life they have reached.

Chapter reflections

» *Reflective practice is an essential component of effective CPD.*

» *The features of reflective practice can be demonstrated at each stage of the CPD process.*

» *Use of a wide variety of sources, including input from others and reference to educational theory, enhances the effectiveness of critical reflection on your CPD.*

Taking it further

Avis, J, Fisher, R and Thompson, P (2010) *Teaching in Lifelong Learning: A Guide to Theory and Practice.* Maidenhead: McGraw Hill Education.

This book contains a detailed section on career planning and CPD.

Hitching, J (2008) *Maintaining Your Licence to Practice.* Exeter: Learning Matters.

This book comprehensively covers the relationship between reflective practice and CPD from the viewpoint of the IfL and contains a host of CPD activities relevant to FE teaching.

References

Brookfield, S (1995) *Becoming Critically Reflective Teachers.* San Francisco: Jossey-Bass.

Dreyfus, S and Dreyfus, H (1980) *A Five-Stage Model of the Mental Activities Involved in Directed Skill Acquisition.* Washington, DC: Storming Media.

Hitching, J (2008) *Maintaining Your Licence to Practice.* Exeter: Learning Matters.

Wallace, S (2007) *Teaching, Tutoring and Training in the Lifelong Learning Sector.* Exeter: Learning Matters.

Websites

www.ifl.ac.uk (last accessed February 2015).

7 Reflective practice: a deeper understanding

What does reflective practice mean?

Reflective practice: a deeper understanding

The wider context of reflective practice

Chapter aims

This chapter will help you to:

- gain a deeper understanding of the terminology and meaning of reflective practice;

- become familiar with current theories of reflective practice;

- develop your own interpretation of reflective practice.

Introduction

The first part of this book has concentrated on the practical aspects of reflective practice. The work of theorists such as Kolb, Schön, Gibbs and Brookfield has been mentioned but only to illustrate specific practical situations. In emphasising the practical experience of teachers as reflective practitioners, we have not asked you to consider in depth what reflective practice actually means.

There is good reason for this. Reflective practice is a contested term with a wide range of definitions dependent on whom you speak to or what books you read. This multiplicity of interpretations has arisen partly because many professions have adopted reflective practice as a key element of their particular brand of professionalism and the term has been interpreted to suit each specific profession. There are also a number of concepts implicit in the term reflective practice, which are themselves open to different interpretations.

This chapter looks in more depth at the interpretations and theoretical basis of reflective practice to help you to gain a deeper understanding of what it means. This should help you develop your own version of the concept and apply it with advantage to your professional (and personal) life.

What does reflective practice mean?

A good starting point to a deeper understanding of reflective practice is to have a look at some of the differing interpretations that are commonly used by people working in the FE sector. Here are a few quotations by FE teachers to illustrate the point.

Renata, food technology teacher, FE College: '*I'm doing reflective practice as part of my Cert Ed. We keep a journal about our experience, not just teaching but also anything else that we think is significant while we are in college. The idea is that we can identify things that go wrong and think of ways of doing it better next time. And we discuss this in tutorials with our personal tutor and our mentor.*'

Paula, Managing Director, large private training agency: '*Yes, reflective practice is a key part of our quality system. After each teaching session all our trainers have to fill in an evaluation form identifying the successful parts of the session and those parts that were problematic, along with thoughts on how they would change things in future. One copy is retained by the trainer as part of their CPD file and another copy goes to the training manager and these are included in the agenda for the progress meetings that every trainer has with the training manager at the end of each month.*'

Khaled, Careers Adviser: '*We studied reflective practice when I did an introduction to counselling course. The counsellor would act rather like a mirror, rephrasing something the client had said so that the words would be reflected back to the client in the hope that they would find a better understanding of their words and the feelings that lay behind them.*'

Matthew, Engineer, industrial trainer: '*Reflective practice? That just means thinking about your teaching, doesn't it? So after you've finished a lesson you might reckon that one part didn't go too well and you'd alter that bit next time you taught that particular lesson. Not exactly rocket science, is it?*'

Clearly such a range of interpretations, varying from simple to complex, can lead to confusion. At its simplest, Matthew sees reflection as little more than casually thinking about an event; at the other extreme, Paula sees reflection as a complex and bureaucratic component of her organisation's quality assurance process. This raises questions around the various meanings of the phrase *reflective practice* and associated terms like *reflection*, *critical reflection* and *reflexivity*. There is need for some clarification.

Reflection

A fairly straightforward interpretation of reflection is the metaphor of a mirror that reflects an accurate image back to you when you look into it. This encourages self-analysis – '*My hair needs cutting*' or '*I look a bit pale*'. In teaching terms, watching a video of a lesson you have taught is the parallel of such a mirror image. This is an interpretation of reflection that is often used in counselling, such as Khaled's experience quoted above. In his case the counsellor acts as the mirror, reflecting the client's statements back by paraphrasing and encouraging the client to re-examine what they actually meant and felt. You may well use this technique of reflection in one-to-one tutorials, getting a learner to re-consider what they have said or written without expressing your own view.

Critical reflection

Reflection can be more than just looking in a mirror. There is the notion of looking *through* a mirror, rather like Alice's discovery in Lewis Carroll's *Through the Looking Glass* when she passes through a mirror and enters a looking-glass world where everything is different. This concept takes you

> ... *right through the mirror's glass to a reflective world where nothing can be taken for granted: everyday actions, events and assumptions about other people take on radically different significance.*

> (Bolton, 2010, p xxi)

As a teacher, reflection in this sense gives you the ability not just to analyse your actions, but to change them so that in future things can be different. Matthew, quoted above, latched on to this when he said, '*you'd alter that bit next time you taught that particular lesson.*' He had identified a problem and was seeking to discover strategies that would solve it. Whenever you decide to try out a couple of new things to solve a teaching problem you are thinking critically, rather than just identifying the problems you have encountered.

> *Critical thinking is a form of discrimination, a way of thinking that is purposeful, producing a considered opinion based on reflection. It gathers information in such a way that you can begin to understand the exact nature of the problem and will in*

turn provide you with the ability to solve problems, make decisions and as a result identify options.

(Roffey-Barentsen and Malthouse, 2009, p 19)

This concept of critical reflection has been thoroughly documented and investigated by a number of writers, starting with John Dewey.

John Dewey

Dewey was one of the first modern authors to write about reflection. Writing in 1933, he interpreted reflection as a method of logical and rigorous thinking that was initiated by someone feeling perplexed by a particular issue. This notion of reflection is more than Matthew's idea of *just thinking* about an issue. Dewey saw reflection as rational, leading to logical solutions that could be tested in practice.

Dewey led the way in emphasising a rational approach to reflection, and the need to be objective and self-critical in analysing issues is an important facet of contemporary reflective practice. There needs to be a systematic approach to reflecting on your practice that enables you to analyse the issues critically and objectively.

Several writers have developed Dewey's ideas of critical reflection and in the last quarter of the twentieth century the idea of using critical reflection to improve performance became very popular. Two of the most influential of these theorists are David Kolb and Graham Gibbs.

David Kolb

You were introduced to the work of David Kolb in Chapter 2, where you saw how his model of experiential learning could be applied to the concept of reflective practice. Using this model, you reflect on and analyse an issue (such as a problem with disruptive learners), research ways of solving the problem (perhaps by reading up about it or discussing it with colleagues) and finally you try out possible alternative strategies.

One of the notable features of Kolb's work is his emphasis on the role that experience plays in learning as distinct from theory, and on the different styles of learning that can be used to reflect on experience. Individuals have different strengths in reflecting: some have strong imaginative ability, some are adept in the practical application of new ideas, some are skilled in creating and interpreting theoretical models and so on. This line of thought has led to considerable literature on learning styles, most notably that of Honey and Mumford (1982) who identified four learning styles. These are:

- *activists – people who learn by doing;*
- *reflectors – people who learn by observing and thinking about experience;*
- *theorists – people who learn from analysing the theory behind issues;*
- *pragmatists – people who learn from experimenting and putting ideas into practice.*

Recently, Honey and Mumford's work has been criticised by some writers as being over-simplistic. However, their concept fits well with Kolb's theory if you link the four learning styles to the four stages of experiential learning. Thus Kolb's concrete experience stage (doing something) is related to activists and his reflective observation stage (thinking about it) has relevance for reflectors. The third stage, abstract conceptualisation (searching for answers), is suited to theorists, and active experimentation (trying out your ideas) is appropriate for pragmatists. The connection can be shown diagrammatically as in Figure 7.1.

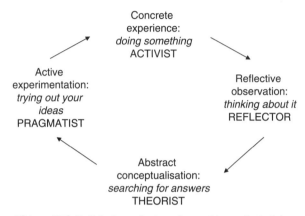

Figure 7.1 *Kolb's learning cycle and learning styles*

The main point of this is that your dominant learning style affects how you reflect. Critical reflection is an individual activity, and there is no one template that will suit everyone. You need to experiment in order to find your preferred learning style and adapt your reflective practice to take this into account.

Critical thinking activity

» *Use the internet and library resources to identify your own dominant learning style. There is a Honey and Mumford questionnaire that you may find useful in doing this.*

» *Select a particular incident and use Kolb's model to reflect critically on it. To what extent is an understanding of your own learning style helpful to your analysis?*

Graham Gibbs

In 1988 Graham Gibbs developed a six-stage model based on Kolb's ideas of experiential learning. These are the stages.

1. **Description**: *'What happened?'*

2. **Feelings**: *'How did you feel?'*

3. **Evaluation**: *'What was good/bad about the experience?'*

4. **Analysis**: *'What sense can you make of the experience?'*

5. **Conclusion**: *'What other action could you have taken?'*

6. **Action plan**: *'What would you do differently next time?'*

This theory is more complex than Kolb's but essentially they both provide a structure for solving teaching problems based on Dewey's concept of reflection as a rational and cyclical process. This is now a very long way from Matthew's idea of *just thinking*. Not only is it purposeful but it is also part of a structured and practical process for dealing with issues which involves discussion with others and use of theory when appropriate.

One aspect to note in Gibbs' model is his emphasis on feelings and emotions, a point we touched upon in Chapter 3. Instead of passing directly from analysis of an event to searching for answers, this model requires you to try and remember how you felt about an event, about the people involved and about the outcome. This can then be compared with your present feelings. Such an exploration from a variety of angles becomes a basis for making an informed judgement about what to do next.

Critical thinking activity

Select an incident that has happened recently in your professional practice. Analyse it in line with Gibbs' reflective cycle, concentrating on your feelings and emotions, by asking yourself questions such as the following.

» *How were you feeling when the incident started?*

» *How did the incident make you feel?*

» *How did those involved make you feel?*

» *What was good about the occurrence?*

» *What was bad about the occurrence?*

Reflexivity

If you imagine a continuum of terms concerning reflective practice that starts with ordinary reflection as the simplest, then reflexivity is likely to be at the other end – the most complex. In essence, reflexivity is critical reflection with an added emphasis of focus on critical *self-reflection*.

> *Reflective practice is learning and developing through examining what we think happened on any occasion, and how we think others perceived the event and us, opening our practice to scrutiny by others, and study texts from the wider sphere. Reflexivity is finding strategies for looking at our own thought processes, values, prejudices and habitual actions, as if we were onlookers.*
>
> (Bolton, 2010, p 7)

In addition to considering their own feelings, reflexive practitioners take into account how their background, environment and beliefs influence their behaviour and this enriches their reflective practice. Take a look back at the chapter on self-awareness, in particular the case studies involving Lin and Paul, and note how these teachers were able to stand outside themselves and observe not just what happened but also to reflect on how and why they acted in a particular way. In terms of Brookfield's critical lenses, this is the ability to turn a critical lens on yourself.

Consequently, reflexivity is not just a matter of identifying new techniques that you can try out to solve problems. You also need to analyse your beliefs and values about teaching, particularly if they were formed in a different educational culture. For example, if your experience of education is a disciplined environment such as the armed forces, you may find that working in an FE college challenges your concept of good teaching and appropriate learner behaviour. If your reflection leads you to adopt a more learner-centred approach, not only because it works but also because it reflects a new philosophy of teaching, you are demonstrating reflexivity. It is a concept that has been covered in the work of several writers. Here is one example.

Chris Johns

Johns' (2000) model for structured reflection was designed with health professionals in mind, but it is equally applicable to education. He sees the most appropriate context for his model as being *guided reflection* with the practitioner maintaining a reflective journal that forms the basis for discussion with an experienced colleague, typically a mentor. In this way reflecting on and sharing experience can lead to deeper understanding than by reflection alone.

Johns envisages two aspects to the reflective process. Firstly, *looking in* involves self-analysis; finding time to identify and write down your feelings and emotions. Secondly, *looking out* concerns reflection on an event. He uses a model designed by Barbara Carper (1978) who classified knowledge and understanding under four headings: aesthetics (What were you trying to do?), personal (What were your feelings?), ethics (Were you acting for the best?) and empirics (What facts did you know?). However, Johns then added a fifth heading: reflexivity. This involves consideration of a number of questions. Here are some examples.

* How does this situation fit in with my ideas about good teaching?

* How does this situation connect with my previous experiences?

* How did the learners perceive the situation and my actions?

* How could I handle the situation better next time?

So for Johns, reflexivity involves the ability to stand outside yourself and to see things from others' points of view. It is about recognising how your values and experiences affect your teaching, and how to record and discuss all this objectively and constructively with others. It is quite a tall order.

Critical thinking activity

» *Using an appropriate search engine, research Johns' model of reflexivity and then apply it to an experience from your own teaching. It would be useful to record your analysis and discuss it with a trusted colleague or mentor.*

Reflective practice

If these notions of reflection, critical analysis and reflexivity are combined and applied to your work as a teacher in FE, this process constitutes reflective practice, a phrase that became well recognised following the publication of Donald Schön's book *The Reflective Practitioner* in 1983.

Donald Schön

Schön's book has become a seminal text for students of reflective practice and you have already considered some of his ideas in earlier chapters. For example, single and double loop learning is included in Chapter 4, and his concept of theories in use and espoused theories is covered in Chapter 5. You have also been introduced to his idea that reflective practice comprises two elements: reflection-on-action and reflection-in-action. It is worth considering these in more detail.

Reflection-on-action is basically thinking about something after the event – the coffee break thoughts after a particularly difficult lesson or discussion with colleagues. Schön also stressed the importance of what he termed *artistry* or reflection-in-action. He saw this as the ability of professionals to improvise, to respond almost instinctively to an unforeseen incident and alter their plans to cope with unexpected situations. The case study involving Penny in the previous chapter illustrates this point.

This is clearly a skill that you do not acquire overnight. It depends on learning from experience rather than a study of theory, and on devising new strategies based on these experiences.

> *The practitioner allows himself to experience surprise, puzzlement, or confusion in a situation which he finds uncertain or unique. He reflects on the phenomenon before him, and on the prior understandings that have been implicit in his behaviour. He carries out an experiment that serves to generate both a new understanding of the phenomenon and a change in the situation.*
>
> (Schön, 1983, p 68)

As you have seen, reflective practice for a probationary teacher is not likely to be the same as that for an experienced teacher. At the start of your career the chances are that you will rely on the experience of others to guide you – educational writers, teacher training tutors, mentors and so on. On the other hand, the experienced teacher has a wealth of experience to draw upon and will have developed their own personal theory of good practice by constantly reflecting on this experience. Schön believed that as professional teachers gain experience and develop their own individual theories so their repertoire of reflecting-in-action skills develop and expand.

Critical thinking activity

» *To what extent do you* reflect-in-action *as distinct from* reflecting-on-action *in your professional practice? What are the implications of Schön's model for your own reflective practice now and in the future?*

Schön's work involving reflective practice has been developed by other writers since publication in the 1980s. Rolfe (2001) provides one example.

Gary Rolfe

Rolfe et al (2001) proposed a model that has the advantage of being easy to understand. They approached reflective practice by using three simple questions to reflect on an issue:

1. **What?**

    This is a trigger to describe in objective terms what actually happened. Subsidiary questions would include:

    • *'What occurred?'*

    • *'What did you do about it?'*

    • *'What was the effect of my actions?'*

2. **So what?**

    The purpose of this question is to gain understanding of the occurrence and construct your own personal theory about what happened. It involves consideration of subsidiary questions like:

    • *'So what does this tell me about my actions?'*

    • *'So what was the effect on my learners?'*

    • *'So what should I have done?'*

3. **Now what?**

    This question is about what changes you need to make in future.

    • *'Now what would I do differently next time?'*

    • *'Now what would be the likely consequences of these changes?'*

Critical thinking activity

» *Select an incident from your recent teaching experience which caused you some difficulty and use Rolfe's model to reflect on it.*

» *To what extent do you find this a useful technique in comparison to the models of reflective practice described in this section?*

The wider context of reflective practice

Corporate reflective practice

So far, the focus in this chapter has been on individual reflective practice; the way in which you develop critical reflection as part of your portfolio of skills as a teacher. However, recent management theory has also included a consideration of reflective practice as an area in which organisations have an important role to play. Vince and Reynolds describe this in the following way:

> *Reflection is an essential part of the day-to-day life of managers, not a disconnected, separate activity but central, supported by structures and the culture of the workplace, affecting decisions and choices, policies and activities and the politics and emotion associated with them. In this way, being reflective will not be understood as a technique, learned and sometimes applied, but an integral part of what it means to lead and to manage.*
>
> (Vince and Reynolds, 2014, p 1)

In this context, reflective practice is seen as an important business strategy, encouraging all staff to reflect on what is and is not working in the organisation. It also creates a structure for appraising, mentoring and providing feedback as employees develop reflective skills to solve problems.

Several writers have developed these ideas. One is Peter Senge (2006) who coined the phrase *learning organisations* to describe those institutions that support critical reflection. Such organisations provide opportunities for team learning, encourage constructive critical discussion and thus facilitate both personal and corporate development. In a learning organisation reflection is a key element of the dialogue between team colleagues that is a driving force of this development.

> *Reflection and inquiry skills provide a foundation for dialogue ... (which) ... is likely to be more reliable and less dependent on particulars of circumstance, such as the chemistry among team members.*
>
> (Senge, 2006, p 249)

This sense that reflective practice can be enriched by sharing and discussing experiences with colleagues is echoed in the work of Etienne Wenger (1998) who argued that learning takes place wherever people get together and relate to one another in what he defined as *communities of practice*. The characteristics of such a community are defined as:

- being committed to the shared interest;

- engaging in joint activities and discussions;

- building relationships so that practitioners can learn from each other;

- creating an environment where practitioners can share experiences and resources;

- being dynamic and involving learning on the part of everyone, whether they are experienced or novices.

Learning in a community of practice involves not only individual reflection but also reflection shared in the community, and Wenger believed that this type of communal reflective practice has unique value. Reed and Canning (2009) make the point that

> *... the reflective practitioner you are now, and the one you will become, has been and will be influenced by the communities in which you learn and practice. The nature of the individuals within these communities and your interaction with them is likely to inform not only your reflective practice but also your identity and self-concept as a reflective practitioner. ... Not only may you see things differently, you may also*

see yourself differently. Participating in a range of communities of learning and practice that offer different perspectives can help us to question and think more clearly about our values, actions and experiences.

(Read and Canning, 2009, p 19)

Critical thinking activity

» *Identify any learning organisations and communities of practice you belong to or have belonged to in the past. To what extent have these environments influenced your reflective practice?*

Professional reflective practice

One consequence of the widespread popularity of reflective practice as an important skill for professional practitioners is that a significant number of professions have identified reflective practice as a key requirement for membership of their occupational groups. This can be illustrated by these extracts from some professional websites (last accessed February 2015).

Chartered Institute of Personnel and Development

Reflection should become a routine part of working life that is more or less instinctive. If you see learning as an intrinsic part of your job, you don't have to interrupt your work to do it. People who routinely plan, record and reflect on their learning tend to see more opportunities for personal development. It's a matter of capturing the moment. The fact is, the world becomes a richer, more stimulating place when you embrace reflective learning, because you switch on a kind of intuitive radar that's tuned to pick up useful opportunities.

www.cipd.co.uk

Chartered Society of Physiotherapists

Reflective practice is a process by which you stop and think about your practice, consciously analyse your decision making and draw on theory and relate it to what you do in practice.

www.csp.org.uk

General Medical Council

You should regularly reflect on your own performance, your professional values and your contribution to any teams in which you work. You should ask for, and be prepared to act on, feedback from colleagues and patients.

www.gmc-uk.org

Chartered Management Institute

It is essential that all managers regularly reflect on how their knowledge and skills need to be updated and plan how they will achieve this. ... It is always a good idea to set some time aside during which you will not be disturbed to think about your professional skills and knowledge as a manager and leader and how you might develop these further to improve your effectiveness.

www.managers.org.uk/

The professions that have taken most interest in encouraging reflective practice tend to be those where personal relationships between professionals and clients are important – professions such as management, health, nursing, social work and not least teaching. All these professions have incorporated critical reflection in their initial training and professional development programmes in recent years. Being reflective is seen as an important element of professionalism, as illustrated by the following quotation from Ray Johnston, a senior manager and director with a lifetime of public service experience.

> *I cannot envisage anyone not routinely reflecting on what they have done, not only in their private but also in their professional life; certainly this is something I always did in those quiet moments, often during the commute at the beginning and end of the working day.*

> *In my experience I found that far too many organisations have a tendency to only look at 'what went wrong as part of the blame game'; a counterproductive mindset which creates a culture where initiative is stifled and individuals are reluctant to put their head above the parapet. A far more creative workplace is one that adopts a 'Plan, Do, Review' methodology where managers and team members look at successful tasks as well as those which foundered.*

Political involvement with reflective practice

It is not just professional bodies and educational theorists that have taken an interest in reflective practice in recent years. Successive governments have adopted policies designed to make a whole range of professions more efficient and accountable. In consequence, there has been a plethora of government initiatives to achieve this aim: introduction of regulatory bodies, control of professional training, nationally defined standards, monitoring of performance through inspection and the power to penalise those professionals who provide inadequate service.

In the case of education this has come in the form of a political agenda in which the primary role of education, particularly vocational education, is seen as training a highly skilled workforce as a key to economic prosperity. The FE sector has been subject to a considerable amount of government regulation designed to ensure high standards of professionalism within the sector, one consequence of which is that reflective practice has become firmly integrated in the list of professional values, skills, knowledge and understanding for all FE teachers working or aspiring to work in the sector.

Government regulation has had a massive effect on the life of teachers in FE. One of these effects has been to change the emphasis of reflective practice from something that FE teachers would do automatically as part of their professional role to something that needs to be backed by regulation to ensure the needs of the organisation and society as a whole are met. This change in emphasis is best seen in the documentation of professional standards for FE teachers. Reflective practice is a key feature of the current set of standards, published by the Education and Training Foundation (ETF) in 2014. For example, the introduction begins with the following words.

> *Teachers and trainers are reflective and enquiring practitioners who think critically about their own educational assumptions, values and practice in the context of a changing contemporary and educational world. They draw on relevant research as part of evidence-based practice.*
>
> (ETF, 2014a, p 1)

Furthermore, top of the list of professional values and attributes is the statement that as a professional teacher you should *reflect on what works best in your teaching and learning to meet the diverse needs of learners* (ETF, 2014a, p 2). The importance of this value is made clear in the guidance notes.

> *The values and attributes described in the Professional Standards are not 'nice to haves'. Rather, they are fundamental, integral and essential to excellent teaching and learning, and supporting learners to be able to reach their full potential.*
>
> *One of the most important feature that identifies excellent teachers and trainers is the extent to which they constantly and critically assess their own performance and practice.*
>
> *Good teachers and trainers also review, on an ongoing basis, their knowledge, assumptions and values against up-to-date professional developments in the world in which they work, drawing on evidence-based practice. They are, therefore, not simply 'aware' of how to teach and understand how learners learn, but do so in a constantly self-appraising manner. Crucially, they are not afraid to admit to developmental needs in any area of their teaching and learning practice, including maths, English and technology knowledge and skills.*
>
> (ETF, 2014b, p 7)

These documents form the basis for including reflective practice in all FE ITT courses, and their curricula are designed to ensure that this is done.

The result of this regulation has been to embed the idea of reflective practice as a key feature of professionalism, whereby FE teachers are required to reflect critically on their work in a much more formalised way, often involving appraisal schemes, formally recording progress and outcomes, sharing with colleagues and using a specific model of reflective practice.

Critical thinking activity

» *Apply the ETF standards relating to reflective practice to analyse how you personally incorporate these activities into your own professional practice.*

Conclusion

Reflective practice is a contested term that involves a number of closely related concepts, all of which have been given slightly different interpretations and emphases by theorists, practitioners and politicians. However, there is a core of agreement that reflective practice is a key skill involving a structured and logical approach to solving professional problems and contributing to effective professional development. This approach involves reflecting on an issue in a rational and non-judgemental way, identifying both positive and negative features, searching for possible solutions, putting the best solution into practice and evaluating the result.

Several factors have influenced the concept of reflective practice such as writers, professional bodies, government policy and regulation. But primarily reflective practice is about you, the teacher, and about enabling you to give your learners the best possible learning experience. Jodi Roffey-Barentsen and Richard Malthouse describe it thus:

> *Reflective practice produces a learner who is autonomous and improves a person's understanding of the subject, and their critical thinking, problem-solving and individual change management skills. ... Reflective practice is used for the purpose of self-improvement ... academically, socially and psychologically.*
>
> (Roffey-Barentsen and Malthouse, 2009, p 9)

This last phrase is significant. The implication is that, although you might adopt reflective practice techniques to improve your professional skills, there is an additional benefit in that you will at the same time improve your social skills and, from a psychological point of view, become a happier and wiser person. This is an assumption that is implicit in the thesis of this book.

Chapter reflections

» *Reflection, critical reflection and reflexivity are key elements of reflective practice.*

» *Reflective practice is a contested term that has been constantly re-interpreted by writers, professions and government organisations in the recent past.*

» *Reflective practice is now a key feature in the training and personal development of many professionals, including teachers in the FE sector.*

» *An understanding of the nature of reflective practice will help you develop your professional skills as a teacher in the FE sector.*

Taking it further

Appleyard, K and Appleyard, N (2014) *The Professional Teacher in Further Education*. Northwich: Critical Publishing.

This is a detailed analysis of professionalism with particular reference to the FE sector. It emphasises the role of critical reflection as an important attribute of professionalism.

Moon, J (2003) *Reflection in Learning and Professional Development.* London: Kogan Page.

This book contains a detailed analysis of what reflective practice actually is. The book reviews current theories of critical reflection and their application to learning and practice.

Kennet, K (2010) Professionalism and Reflective Practice, in Wallace, S (ed) *The Lifelong Learning Sector Reflective Reader.* Exeter: Learning Matters.

This article reviews the theory of reflective practice and the issues of putting the theoretical concepts into practice.

References

Bolton, G (2010) *Reflective Practice, Writing and Professional Development.* London: Sage Publications.

Carper, B (1978) Fundamental Patterns of Knowing in Nursing. *Advances in Nursing Science* 1(1): 13–24.

Dewey, J (1933) *How We Think. A Restatement of the Relation of Reflective Thinking to the Educative Process.* Boston: D C Heath.

ETF (2014a) *Professional Standards for Teachers and Trainers in Education and Training – England.* London: Education and Training Foundation.

ETF (2014b) *Initial Guidance for Users of the Professional Standards for Teachers and Trainers in Education and Training – England.* London: Education and Training Foundation.

Gibbs, G (1988) *Learning by Doing: A Guide to Teaching and Learning Methods.* Oxford: Oxford Polytechnic Further Education Unit.

Honey, P and Mumford, A (1982) *Manual of Learning Styles,* London: Peter Honey Publications.

Institute for Learning (2007) *Guidelines for Your Continuing Professional Development (CPD).* London: IfL.

Johns, C (2000) *Becoming a Reflective Practitioner: A Reflective & Holistic Approach to Clinical Nursing, Practice Development & Clinical Supervision.* Oxford: Blackwell Science.

Kolb, D (1983) *Experiential Learning.* Englewood Cliffs, New Jersey: Prentice-Hall.

Reed, M and Canning, N (2009) *Reflective Practice in the Early Years.* London: Sage Publications Ltd.

Roffey-Barentsen, J and Malthouse, R (2009) *Reflective Practice in the Lifelong Learning Sector.* Exeter: Learning Matters.

Rolfe, G et al (2001) *Critical Reflection for Nursing and the Helping Professions.* Basingstoke: Palgrave Macmillan.

Schön, D (1983) *The Reflective Practitioner: How Professionals Think in Action.* New York: Basic Books.

Senge, P (2006) *The Fifth Discipline: The Art and Practice of the Learning Organisation.* London: Random House.

Vince, R and Reynolds, M (2014) *Organising Reflective Practice.* www2.warwick.ac.uk (last accessed February 2015).

Wenger, E (1998) *Communities of Practice: Learning, Meaning and Identity.* Cambridge: Cambridge University Press.

Websites

www.cipd.co.uk (accessed February 2015).

www.csp.org.uk (accessed February 2015).

www.et-foundation.co.uk (accessed February 2015).

www.gmc-uk.org (accessed February 2015).

www.managers.org.uk (accessed February 2015).

www2.warwick.ac.uk (accessed February 2015).

8 Evaluating reflective practice: benefits and limitations

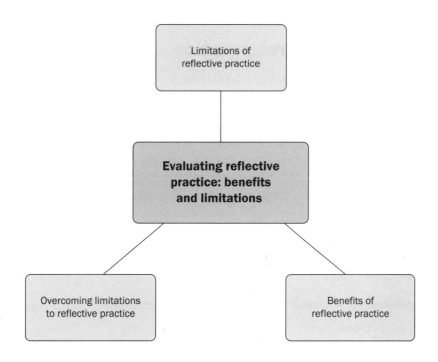

Chapter aims

This chapter will help you to:

- identify the limitations of reflective practice;
- develop strategies for overcoming these limitations in your own reflective practice;
- review the benefits of reflective practice.

Introduction

The concept of reflective practice as a fundamental and essential skill for FE teachers is now so ubiquitous within the FE sector that it is often accepted without question as a good thing. Linda Finlay makes the point that:

> ... reflective practice is a desirable, foundational dimension of professional action and lifelong learning is often taken as self-evident. Whether the rhetoric emanates from colleagues, professional bodies, educators, management, or the government, practitioners are forever being exhorted to reflect and to critically evaluate their performance.
>
> (Finlay, 2008, p 10)

However, there are limitations that need to be recognised when applying the concept of reflective practice to the FE sector. This chapter evaluates some of these issues and suggests ways they may be overcome, before reviewing the benefits of reflective practice that have been implicit in the previous chapters of this book.

Limitations of reflective practice

A major theme of this book is that reflective practice is potentially very rewarding. This does not mean that it is easy; it has significant problems, as Finlay (2008) summarises in the following extract.

> The problem with reflective practice is that it is hard to do. ...This is hardly surprising given the confusion about what exactly it is, the complexity of the processes involved and the fact that there is no end to what can be reflected upon. ... In addition, reflective practice is highly context specific. Each individual practitioner will need to reflect in different ways at different times. And different contexts (environment, organisation and relational) will demand different sorts of reflecting.
>
> (Finlay, 2008, p 14)

This section considers some of these issues, including:

- the bureaucratic consequences of organisational demands;
- problems of context;
- confusion of terminology;
- introspection and isolation.

Bureaucracy and reflective practice

One problematic effect of efforts to professionalise the FE workforce through the introduction of mandatory professional standards has been to create an environment in which reflective practice can be seen as a tedious chore to be completed in order to provide evidence for regulatory bodies and college managers that something is being done. This has been documented by several writers.

The growth of managerialism and the audit culture fuels demands for evidence to demonstrate reflective practice. Consequently, reflection is often used as a 'tool' for personal and professional development, and professionals are expected to produce some sort of written reflective record. … Furthermore, the reflections themselves can be superficial and procedural as if one was following a recipe compliantly, rather than questioning and challenging. Reflection … becomes a tool for control and orthodoxy.

(Kilminster, in Bradbury et al, 2010, p 3)

Reflection can be turned into recipe-following checklists which students work through in a mechanical fashion without regard to their own uncertainties, questions and meanings.

(Boud, Keogh and Walker, 1998, p 193)

Busy, over-stretched professionals are likely to find reflective practice taxing and difficult. Bland, mechanical, routinised and unthinking ways of doing reflective practice are too often the result. … Students may develop considerable antagonism towards their reflective assignments, which they view as having no intrinsic meaning. Students tend to adopt a minimalist approach, writing just enough to meet the requirement for a pass or even writing fictionalised accounts of idealised practice.

(Finlay, 2008, pp 10, 14)

In an environment where you are constantly under pressure, coping with a heavy administrative load and dealing with difficult teaching situations, it is not surprising that finding time to reflect and record your conclusions is accorded a low priority, resulting in some of the attitudes described above.

The good news is that following the Lingfield report and the revocation of the 2007 regulations, there is now a possibility that reflective practice in FE, instead of being seen as an externally imposed requirement forming part of a mandatory ITT qualification or CPD programme, can be owned by practitioners themselves and negotiated locally. If this is so, there is a chance that the *tick box* and routinised approaches may become less prevalent in the sector.

Critical thinking activity

» *To what extent do you feel that the introduction of professional standards and government regulation has affected your ability to develop as a reflective practitioner? Give examples from your own experience as a practising teacher.*

Problems of context

The opportunities you have to develop your skills of critical reflection depend on your professional context – where you work. David Boud (in Bradbury et al, 2010) stresses this point.

Practice always occurs in a particular setting … The people involved vary, the influences of the organisation vary and power relations vary. This means that

> *any standardised approach to reflection must be treated with great caution ... The tailoring of reflection to suit local settings follows from a recognition of the importance of context (and) reflection must be designed for context. It must take into account the particularities of the setting and accommodate the actual people involved and the practice that is being reflected upon.*
>
> (Bradbury et al, 2010, pp 33–4)

Additionally, a notable feature of FE is its diversity, as illustrated in the following quotation from the Lingfield report.

> *The sector consists of 244 general FE colleges, 94 sixth form colleges (largely funded by the EFA), 15 specialist designated institutions (for example, Ruskin College and the City Lit.), over 1,000 private or charitable training providers, over 200 public bodies such as local authorities offering adult community learning, 38 HE institutions which also offer FE courses, 18 National Skills Academies, the training departments of major employers such as Rolls-Royce and Jaguar Land Rover, 14 NHS Trusts, government departments such as the Ministry of Defence, the armed services and government agencies like the Prison Service.*
>
> (BIS, 2012, p 18)

Such diversity means that inevitably there will be considerable local variation in the way that individual institutions view reflective practice. You may be working in a large institution that has a sophisticated quality assurance system that offers considerable support for reflective practice at one extreme, or in a small organisation that does not have the resources to do this at the other. In this circumstance, the responsibility for your professional development as a reflective practitioner falls to a much greater extent on your own motivation and commitment. However, no matter where you work, if your reflective practice is to be effective you need to know your organisation in order to work out how you can best develop your reflective skills within it.

Critical thinking activity

» *How is reflective practice supported and resourced in your organisation? Your analysis may include such support features as:*

» *appraisal schemes with a developmental focus;*

» *provision and training of mentors for newly appointed teachers;*

» *staff training;*

» *quality assurance systems.*

» *Evaluate the extent to which this context facilitates your development as a reflective practitioner.*

Confusion of terminology

The fact that the term *reflective practice* has different meanings for different people was considered briefly in the previous chapter. This confusion can cause problems, well described by one ITT learner.

It's all very well for my tutor to suggest reading a whole list of books about reflective practice, but when I started I got really confused about the language. I don't have an academic background and so having to cope with words that are used in different ways by different writers adds an extra layer of difficulty. Why can't we have one definition of things like 'critical reflection', 'reflexivity', 'reflection in action', 'espoused theories' and so on so that everyone knows what we are talking about?

John (electrical installations teacher at FE college, attending part-time DTL course)

The perplexity that John is expressing here is all too common. Many writers have expressed similar criticism as shown by the following quotations.

The lack of clarity and consensus is the most frequently raised critique about reflective practice. … In short, there is no agreement on what reflective practice is … In the present article we refer to 'reflective practice', whereas other authors prefer 'reflexivity', 'reflection', 'reflective analysis' and so on. On the other hand, some authors use the same term but refer to considerably different concepts of reflective practice. To date, there is no consistent correspondence between the terms used and the meanings implied.

(Collin et al, 2013, p 7)

The ambiguity of the term 'reflective practice' continues with its lack of standard definition. Other popular terms such as 'critical thinking', 'critical reflection' and 'reflection' per se are overlappingly and interchangeably used with reflective practice. … The lack of clear or universal definitions of reflection (has) resulted in confusion about its meaning and its uses.

(Cheldelin et al, 2004, p 13)

It seems that this situation of confusing terminology is a consequence of the considerable popularity of the concept of reflective practice since Schön and Kolb published their seminal works. Many professions have adopted reflective practice as a key theme of their interpretation of professionalism and they have done so in different ways. Even if you confine yourself to researching educational literature, you will have no difficulty in finding a wide range of books on the subject with different usage of terminology.

The key to managing this difficulty lies in the realisation that your style of reflection is unique. This involves deciding for yourself what precisely the technical terms associated with reflective practice mean to you, so that you can develop your own practice in ways that suit your own professional situation, skills and experience.

Critical thinking activity

» *Review the literature and note the different interpretations of key words associated with reflective practice. You may find it useful to compare these interpretations with the terminology used in your own organisation.*

Introspection and isolation

> *Reflective practice leaves me feeling somewhat raw and exposed when I realise I have weaknesses that I hadn't considered.*
>
> (Darren, part-time teacher studying for PGCE)

> *I tend to be ultra-critical, so sometimes reflective practice makes me feel bad.*
>
> (Wendy, hairdressing teacher studying for ATL)

> *Reflection sometimes helps me but can also pull you down if you're not in the correct frame of mind. Sometimes you need another person to point things out and give some help.*
>
> (Sarah, employability skills teacher studying for DTL)

These quotations illustrate another potential limitation to effective reflective practice, whereby the process is seen as an essentially individual activity and consequently is not effectively supported. There is no doubt that much of the early writing on reflective practice emphasised an individualistic view of learning and many ITT courses have been designed on the basis of individual and autonomous professional practice.

One problem with this approach is that it can lead to feelings of inadequacy and self-disapproval arising when the going gets tough. If teachers feel isolated and interpret critical reflection in a negative way, reflective practice can become a depressing rather than a liberating activity. The danger is that negativity will dominate their reflections unless they can get constructive help and support.

Critical thinking activity

» *What advice would you give to the three teachers quoted in this section to develop their reflective techniques in a more constructive way?*

Overcoming limitations to reflective practice

Limitations such as administrative bureaucracy, confusion of terminology and negative introspection mean that putting your beliefs about reflection into practice may be more difficult than you think initially. However, there are ways of mitigating these problems. Consider the experience of Martyn in the following case study.

CASE STUDY

Martyn's reflections

Martyn is an experienced FE teacher who is encountering some difficulty in putting his beliefs into practice, as shown by this extract from his reflective journal.

Looking back over the past semester, I'm beginning to realise that I'm not as conscientious a practitioner as I'd like to be. When I did my Cert Ed five years ago I was a real enthusiast for reflecting on my teaching, discussing problems with my mentor, keeping a journal and all the other components of reflective practice. I was keen to keep this up after I qualified because I could see that it made me a more sensitive and better teacher.

The trouble is that over the past couple of years all these good intentions have increasingly stayed like that – just intentions and not actually doing very much. I haven't kept up my journal regularly and rarely have time to discuss things with any of my colleagues. And I'm feeling guilty about it, because I am still a firm believer in critical reflection as a way of developing as a better teacher. Of course, I can think of lots of good reasons why I haven't kept things going: lack of time, dozens of meetings, a big marking load and many other hindrances that get in the way of reflecting. But fundamentally, I'm beginning to wonder if these are just excuses. If I really believed that reflective practice was so important, then I'd make sure I found the time to do it properly.

Critical thinking activity

»   *What tactics could Martyn adopt to retain the level of involvement in reflective practice that he experienced during his teacher training?*

What Martyn is expressing here is the difficulty of actually putting into practice something that he sincerely believes in. He says that he thinks reflective practice is a good thing but does not actually do it. In Schön's terminology there is a mismatch between his espoused theory (what he says he believes in) and his theory in use (what he actually does), and there is good evidence that this is not an uncommon experience for teachers. Kennet (in Wallace, 2010, pp 74–5) quotes studies that found that less than 10 per cent of teachers actually fully integrated reflective practice into their teaching and in another study only 10 per cent followed a cyclical reflective process. Clearly, there is need for some strategies to turn a belief in the importance of reflective practice into actually doing it.

Getting help from others

One of the most useful of these strategies is to get help from others, as you have seen from a number of case studies in this book. Focusing on the individual nature of reflective practice, seeing reflection as predominantly a personal rather than a social activity can inhibit this approach but the emphasis on individual autonomy has lessened in recent years. For example, Etienne Wenger's ideas on communities of practice, discussed in the previous chapter, make the point that learning takes place wherever people get together and relate to one another in a professional environment.

This does not mean that there is no place for quiet and solitary reflection. It does mean, however, that involving others in your reflective practice has several benefits in addition to reducing the negative effects of a tendency to navel gazing. Warwick (2007) argues strongly for

… reflection as a social practice, in which the articulation of ideas to others is central to the development of a critical perspective and so to the development of appreciative systems. In short, we all need a mentor.

(Warwick, 2007, p 5)

If you are studying for a teaching qualification, the chances are that a mentor, or at least a personal tutor, will be available to help you and guide your reflective practice. But there is no reason why you should limit yourself to obtaining support from these colleagues. There is normally a variety of help available to enrich your reflective practice whether you are a novice or an experienced teacher. The argument here is for what is known as a dialogic approach. Put in simple terms, you may be able to avoid or overcome any possible negative feelings that follow from reflecting on a problem such as a lesson that did not work by discussing it with others – colleagues, managers, tutors and so forth.

Using formal support mechanisms

It may well be that your organisation has several mechanisms that can provide the means to support your reflective practice. One consequence of government efforts to professionalise the FE workforce has been to put pressure on employers to establish quality assurance systems that provide support for teachers to gain qualifications, to keep up to date and to strive for excellence throughout their professional careers. Thus regulatory bodies such as QAA and Ofsted place considerable emphasis on seeing evidence of systems that improve the quality of teaching and this inevitably involves encouraging reflective practice.

Consequently, many colleges and other FE institutions have now developed processes that will ensure that teachers like Martyn do not feel isolated in their efforts to develop their skills as reflective practitioners. A good example of this trend is the experience of Boston College in Lincolnshire where a range of college-wide support systems to improve the quality of teaching and learning have been introduced in recent years.

The college management's approach to raising teaching standards across the college has been to work towards creating a Wenger-style community of practice. To this end, the college has:

- appointed advanced practitioners (APs) to act as mentors, to conduct lesson observations and to help develop the quality of the learning and teaching across the college;

- opened a teaching and learning hub (TLH) to act as a focal point to train teachers and promote good teaching and learning. Staffed by the members of the college quality assurance scheme and the APs, the TLH has proved extremely popular as a central point where staff can obtain support to improve their teaching practice with access to a wide range of materials and the opportunity to discuss issues with colleagues and the TLH staff;

- introduced both formal and informal teaching observation processes administered through the TLH. These include peer group observations within a *teaching triangle* initiative in which groups of three teachers from different curriculum areas observe each others' teaching. This has proved a very effective way of sharing best practice;

- established a support network of teachers who aim to attain an *outstanding* Ofsted grading. The activities of this network, called J20 (Journey to Outstanding) include regular network meetings to share best practice, developmental observations, one-to-one coaching and two-way reflection with an allocated J20 link person.

Taken together, these initiatives are in line with Senge's (2006) writing about learning oganisations, in which he emphasises the importance of organisational support structures that will enrich the development of individual reflective practice. This is a trend that is evident in many FE institutions as the pressure to improve the standard of teaching and learning increases, and potentially such support structures can be used to overcome the limitations to effective reflective practice that led to the disconnection between Martyn's espoused theory and his theory in use.

Critical thinking activity

» *Compare the above support system to the support system in your own organisation.*

Benefits of reflective practice

There is no doubt that many FE teachers become involved with reflective practice somewhat reluctantly and only realise the benefits at a later date. A typical situation is where being reflective and recording conclusions is something you have to do as part of an ITT course or a college quality assurance scheme. In these circumstances it is not surprising if the whole process is initially regarded with some scepticism, as seen from the following quotation from Lana, who is attending a DTL course.

> When we were first told that we had to keep a reflective journal throughout the course I thought that it was going to be a real pain. I didn't see the point, and more importantly I was sure that I didn't have the time. It's stressful enough trying to do my job – teaching, meetings, assessment, etc, etc – and cope with the DTL without having to fill in masses of extra paperwork every week.
>
> It was only after I reached the end of the course that I realised how much critical reflection had helped me understand myself and my learners. I think it has helped me become better at my job.
>
> (Lana, community care teacher, NHS trust)

You may initially be extrinsically motivated in a similar fashion to Lana, feeling that reflecting is something you have to do in order to gain a qualification. In other words, you make the best of a tedious job. However, once you begin to reflect, you may well realise that, notwithstanding all the limitations, a whole range of intrinsic benefits accrue if you commit time and effort to becoming a reflective practitioner. Many of these intrinsic benefits are implicit throughout earlier chapters, but it may be helpful to review them here in more detail.

Finding solutions to problems you experience in your teaching

Structured reflection and making notes in a journal about critical incidents enables you to analyse them in an objective way and to think of possible solutions that you can try out in future lessons. Additionally, you capture insights that can be revisited when you review your journal at a later date.

Identifying your personal strengths and building on them

Reflective practice encourages self-awareness and the ability to identify your strengths, value your own knowledge and develop your creative talents. Identifying the good feelings you experience when a lesson goes well helps to build your confidence and self-esteem.

Identifying your personal weaknesses and finding strategies to mitigate them

A more uncomfortable aspect of self-knowledge is having to recognise characteristics that mitigate against successful teaching. However, willingness to look at all your personality traits dispassionately means that you will be better able to accept challenging situations and to deal with them more effectively.

Improving your organisational, problem-solving and decision-making skills

A systematic approach to reflection contributes to effective organisational skills, including planning and evaluation. The ability to identify significant incidents, record these events in a journal and think of ways you might improve requires a logical routine and finding the time to reflect effectively. Such an approach is equally valid for solving a variety of problems and for making effective decisions, not necessarily restricted to your professional role.

A greater awareness of the beliefs and values that guide actions

Reflective practice gives you a deeper understanding of the beliefs and values that guide your actions and helps you to recognise and understand the beliefs and values held by your learners and colleagues.

Improving your personal and professional relationships with learners and colleagues

Getting together with others for a chat and to share information is another benefit. Tutors, colleagues and mentors can give advice and this alone goes a long way to establishing good professional relationships. In addition, a willingness to obtain feedback from your learners is likely to improve your relationships with them.

Keeping up to date and developing as a professional who is constantly learning

Keeping up to date implies a desire to be a perennial learner. You will need to search the internet, use the library, and read books and journals. Of course, you know this because this is exactly what you are doing now – reading about reflective practice.

Being professional means that developing your skills of critical reflection is a career-long process, and this aspect is constantly emphasised in the literature on reflective practice. For example, Peter Tarrant writes:

Through reflecting on our practice, we become more aware, more in control, more able to see our strengths and development needs. Through reflection, we can begin to move from novice to expert. … Indeed, it helps the expert to continue and grow and develop. It may even enable the expert to pass on this expertise to other professionals as they share their reflection.

(Tarrant, 2013, p 2)

In summary, Lana's quotation illustrates a fairly common change of attitude. She started by feeling she had to study reflective practice because it was an ITT course requirement. She finished with a better understanding of her own values, beliefs and emotions and how this helps her teaching. She is beginning to experience what several writers have called the emancipatory benefits in which

… you take control over your professional practice in the knowledge that you cannot change everything but you accept that there are some things you can change. As a result, the experience becomes emancipatory; in other words, it liberates you.

(Roffey-Barentsen and Malthouse, 2009, p 24)

Critical thinking activity

»   *The list of benefits in this section is not exhaustive and some will resonate with you more than others, depending on your experience, personality and professional situation. To what extent are the benefits listed above evident in your own professional practice? What examples from your recent practice can you identify to illustrate your conclusions?*

Conclusion

There is no doubt that the practical and philosophical limitations of reflective practice can mitigate against its effectiveness and make the aim that FE '*teachers and trainers are reflective and enquiring practitioners who think critically about their own educational assumptions, values and practice*' (ETF, 2014, p 1) difficult to achieve. However, there are ways of overcoming the limitations and the benefits are considerable and worth the effort.

Effective reflective practice is not an easy option; it requires a high level of intrinsic motivation. The key to whether it is effective lies in how well it is done. If it is mechanistic, poorly supported and becomes routinised, the chances are that the limitations will become prevalent and reflective practice will be seen as just another externally imposed burden on overworked teachers. On the other hand, if it is well supported, encourages critical self-awareness and a structured and logical approach, the potential for personal and corporate benefit is considerable.

Several writers have suggested that action research might be a valuable step in developing your skills as a reflective practitioner, and this is the focus of the next chapter.

Chapter reflections

» *There are limitations to reflective practice. These include confusing terminology, the bureaucratic effects of regulation and the pressures of working in the diverse and demanding FE sector.*

» *Seeking advice from others and making use of formal quality assurance processes in your organisation can be effective ways of dealing with these limitations.*

» *There are substantial benefits to continuing to develop your skills as a reflective practitioner throughout your career as a professional FE teacher.*

Taking it further

Bradbury, H et al (2010) *Beyond Reflective Practice: New Approaches to Professional Lifelong Learning.* Abingdon: Routledge.

This book comprises a collection of articles that critically examine the concept and application of reflective practice, offering a range of perspectives and insights into contemporary views.

Finlay, L (2008) *Reflecting on 'Reflective Practice'* PBPL paper 52. A Discussion Paper prepared for PBPL CETL.

This is a detailed critique of reflective practice, highlighting the dangers of applying the concept mechanistically and suggesting approaches that will encourage effective critical reflection.

References

BIS (2012) *Professionalism in Further Education – Final Report.* London: BIS.

Boud, D, Keogh, R and Walker, D (1985) *Reflection: Turning Experience into Learning.* London: Kogan Page.

Bradbury, H, Frost, N, Kilminster, S and Zukas, M (2010) *Beyond Reflective Practice: New Approaches to Professional Lifelong Learning.* Abingdon: Routledge.

Cheldelin, S, Makamba, J and Warfield, W (2004) *Reflections on Reflective Practice.* Paper submitted to ICAR Winter 2004 Conference. [online] Available at: scar.gmu.edu/Reflective%20Practice.pdf (accessed February 2015).

Collin, S, Karsenti, T and Komis, V (2013) Reflective Practice in Initial Teacher Training: Critiques and Perspective. *Reflective Practice: International and Multidisciplinary Perspectives,* 14 (1): 104–17.

ETF (2014) *Professional Standards for Teachers and Trainers in Education and Training – England.* London: Education and Training Foundation.

Finlay, L (2008) *Reflecting on Reflective Practice.* PBPL paper 52: A Discussion Paper prepared for PBPL CETL. [online] Available at: www.open.ac.uk/pbpl (accessed February 2015).

Kennet, K (2010) Professionalism and Reflective Practice, in Wallace, S (eds) *The Lifelong Learning Sector Reflective Reader.* Exeter: Learning Matters.

Roffey-Barentsen, J and Malthouse, R (2009) *Reflective Practice in the Lifelong Learning Sector.* Exeter: Learning Matters.

Senge, P (2006) *The Fifth Discipline: The Art and Practice of the Learning Organisation.* London: Random House.

Tarrant, P (2013) *Reflective Practice and Professional Development.* London: Sage.

Warwick, P (2007) *Reflective Practice: Some Notes on the Development of the Notion of Professional Reflection.* ESCalate (Education Subject Centre of the Higher Education Academy). [online] Available at: http://dera.ioe.ac.uk/id/eprint/13026 (accessed February 2015).

Websites

scar.gmu.edu/Reflective%20Practice.pdf (accessed February 2015).

http://dera.ioe.ac.uk/id/eprint/13026 (accessed February 2015).

www.open.ac.uk/pbpl (accessed February 2015).

9 Reflection in action research

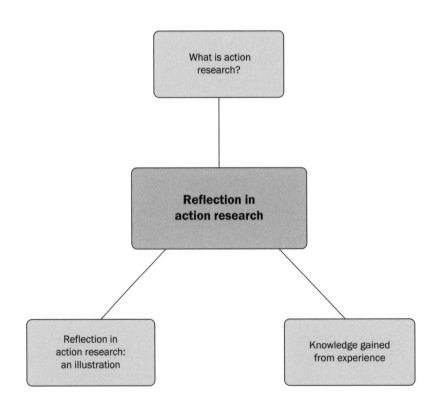

What is action
research?

Reflection in
action research

Reflection in
action research:
an illustration

Knowledge gained
from experience

Chapter aims

This chapter will help you to:

* understand what action research is and be aware of different theories and approaches;

* recognise reflection as an essential element in action research;

* engage in action research as a reflective practitioner to enhance your professional and personal life.

Introduction

Hear or read the word *research* and you might think of hours spent in a library reading lengthy texts, making copious notes and writing a report with an abstract, an analysis of data and so on. This is a fairly typical image of research but action research is different. There are two reasons for this difference. Firstly, you choose to do the action research you want to and to do it when you want to: you choose what you are going to research and the way you are going to do it. Secondly, it is research into action. Although you will gain from background reading, the focus is on action – your action mainly, but also the actions of those around you. This chapter is about engaging in action research and more specifically about the reflection that has such a major role to play in it.

The chapter opens with a brief overview of some of the features and theories of action research and the different approaches to it. It continues by re-introducing Kolb's model of experiential learning before moving on to an in-depth case study that illustrates the role of reflection in action research.

What is action research?

The first point to note about action research is that it does not appear in the garb of *one size fits all*. Nor does the way you set about doing it: indeed it encompasses a range of different theories and approaches and has been defined in many different ways. Here are three of those definitions.

Action research:

* *is an enquiry which is carried out in order to understand, to evaluate and then to change, in order to improve educational practice* (Bassey, 1998, p 93);

* *involves practitioners in studying their own professional practice and framing their own questions. Their research has the immediate goal to assess, develop or improve their practice* (Zeni, 1998, p 13 cited in www.open.ac.uk/cobe/docs/AR-Guide-final);

* *is simply a form of self-reflective enquiry undertaken by participants in social situations in order to improve the rationality and justice of their own practices, their understanding of these practices and the situations in which the practices are carried out* (Carr and Kemmis, 1986, p 162).

Theories and approaches

Kurt Lewin (1946) was the first to use the term action research, describing it as a spiral of steps. Probably the best way to visualise his idea is to imagine a spiral staircase. Each circle of the staircase contains the same group of steps; a fact finding step, a planning step, an action step, an evaluating step, an amended plan step, and then another action step and so on. You will likely have already noticed the similarity of Lewin's model to the cyclical and ongoing features of reflective practice.

Lawrence Stenhouse (1975) wrote about the role of teachers in engaging in the research process. He took the approach that teachers should be active in researching their own practice; indeed he believed they were the best equipped to do so. He suggested that by taking on the role of a detached, objective researcher they would gain greater control of their own practice. An important theme of Stenhouse's approach was teacher autonomy. Others such as, for example, John Elliott (1991) and Carr and Kemmis (1986) extended Stenhouse's ideas and worked to give action research a strong focus within the teaching profession.

Approaches to action research have developed in different ways so that some focus on the validity of the results, others on the methods and process or technical aspects, yet others on the values that inform action. Despite these differences, action research can be characterised by a number of core features.

Features

Reflection

Reflection is at the heart of action research. At every stage you reflect on what is happening, you question, you search for a way forward and – following action – you look again and question again.

Action

Action in this context is everyday action, the ongoing things you do and the experiences you have on a daily basis, particularly the interactions you have with those around you.

Collaboration

Action research involves others in what you are doing. It is about how you learn through engaging with others, by listening, negotiating and working together to understand each other's point of view and to share knowledge.

Empowerment

Action research is often described as emancipating or empowering. It encourages autonomy and responsibility, and is a mandate for creativity and inventiveness. Furthermore, the experience of engaging in it opens the way to new learning and knowledge.

Models relating to action research

Action research, just like reflective practice itself, is sometimes presented through models. However good the action research model is, it will have limitations, even if it is simply the danger of providing too rigid an idea of what action research is. Yet a model can give you the technical framework for reflection and action, provided it is seen in a supporting role. David Boud (2010) makes this point when writing about the value of using a framework. Reflecting, suggests Boud,

> ... is a means to engage in making sense of experience in situations that are rich and complex and which do not lend themselves to being simplified by the use of concepts and frameworks that can be taught. This does not, however, mean that concepts and frameworks have no part to play in reflecting. Quite the contrary, these are needed not to recall and regurgitate but to help prompt and make sense of the complexity of experience.
>
> (Boud, 2010, p 29)

One model that you might find helpful, and one that is relevant to reflection in action research, is Kolb's experiential learning cycle. You were introduced to Kolb's model in earlier chapters. The four stages of the cycle (concrete experience, reflective observation, abstract conceptualisation and active experimentation) provide a useful framework for the cyclical and ongoing nature of reflection in action research. Jennifer Moon suggests that:

> ... the Kolb cycle mirrors processes of problem solving, creativity and research and the sequence has become closely associated with the process of action research.
>
> (Moon, 2010, p 35)

Moon goes on to suggest that the cycle demonstrates the dual role of reflection in action research.

> Reflection in action research appears to have two stated roles. The first is to form the basis for the planned action, where there is reflection on the meaning of the observations of an event or a situation in order to plan the action. The second, which takes place after the action, is to evaluate the problems and effects of the action. Reflection is retrospective in both phases of the cycle. In the one it concerns, the nature of the situation that stimulates the planning of action and in the second it provides the basis for evaluating action already taken but will also form the basis for new action if more action is envisaged.
>
> (Moon, 2010, p 37)

Reflection in action research: an illustration

In the following illustration of reflection in action research you will be able to observe the four stages of Kolb's learning cycle as well as reflection in both the roles that Moon describes: as the basis for planned action and as a means of evaluating the effects of the action.

CASE STUDY

Kate's action research project

Kate teaches business skills on a part-time basis at an inner-city FE college. She undertakes action research aimed at developing ways to improve the communication between herself and her learners and between her learners themselves. The following series of extracts taken from Kate's journal illustrates her experience of reflection as she undertakes her action research project.

Extract one: reflecting on choices, planning and feelings

In this first extract Kate describes how and why she has decided to undertake an action research project. She reflects on how she feels about doing this type of research and on possible planning options.

I have been teaching now for three years and believe that action research is going to help me to develop my practice. I began reflecting on my teaching when I was working towards DTTLS. But I am keen to be more proactive and it feels like the right time. Choosing a topic took a little thought. There were lots of ideas going round in my head so I decided to have a word with Mira my line manager and she has helped me clear my mind.

I am interested in how we interact with each other, especially how the way we communicate affects others. I think communication is vitally important and is sometimes overlooked. How you feel is obviously likely to have an effect on what you say and how you say it. If you are enthusiastic hopefully it's contagious; if you are feeling irritated that too is going to rub off on learners and colleagues alike. But I was thinking also of the small things, the things we do that we might not even be aware of, things we say without thinking and even things that show up in our body language. I think we just get a bit lazy and get into bad habits that are hard to break unless you make the effort. I'm sure there is always potential for improvement so my research is going to be into how we, that is my group of learners and myself, can improve our communication with each other.

I feel excited about doing this research, partly because the topic itself genuinely interests me, partly because I believe that we are all going to benefit from doing it, but it's also because this is my project. I am the one who has decided to do it. I remember doing a research project when I was training and it was OK – I quite enjoyed it in fact, but this is different, this is something I am doing for myself to improve and develop my teaching. I really value this sense of freedom about what I do and how I do it.

I want to keep my project simple because I'm feeling my way. I have started to jot down some ideas and have begun working on a concept map of possibilities. I need to work out how I can gather the information I need. Perhaps I could design a simple questionnaire for my learners to record their thoughts and feelings on how we communicate with each other and any suggestions they may have. I think this is a good option. It means I will have a written record of what they say. A second option might be to have a brainstorming session to start with. This would be more relaxed and spontaneous and I do want them to feel it is something they can be very much involved in and enjoy doing. The questionnaires could then be completed as backup and would prove useful for them to record anything they may not feel confident to say in class.

Another option would be for me to do a video recording so we could all see what happens in a typical session, but there is a problem here. If I tell them why I'm recording, they may well be nervous and clam up, on the other hand it seems dishonest not to say why, so I don't think this is going to work.

The same might be said for asking Mira to come and sit in on a session to observe how we all communicate with each other and then give us some feedback – they are going to feel like insects under the microscope. On the other hand, Mira might be able to give me some feedback on how I communicate with my learners. She knows me pretty well and there have been lots of occasions when she's been around when I have been interacting with learners. So that's a definite. My first step is to talk to my group, tell them I'd like their help in working together to improve our communication with each other and ask them what they think.

Kate had a number of ideas going around in her head and looked to her line manager for help in clearing her mind. Even at this early stage in her action research she understood that collaborating with a colleague is going to be of value. She decides to keep her action research project small and simple as it is a new experience for her. This is probably a wise move. When you undertake an action research project you are to some extent out on a limb. You do not know what will happen. On the other hand, it provides an opportunity to be creative and inventive, to try out ideas and see what happens and, as Kate discovered, this autonomy gives a sense of freedom. She begins to reflect on planning, jotting ideas down in the form of a concept map, considering the advantages and disadvantages of different options. But it is reflecting on her knowledge of her learners and on her observations of the situation that helps her to plan how she will set about her research. She knows that there is potential for improvement in communication and she also knows her learners will respond best to a project which is relaxed and fun and one that they feel involved in.

Critical thinking activity

Reflect on an action research project you would like to undertake. You might find the following questions helpful.

» *Do you feel that an action research project would be appropriate for you to do now?*

» *What topics or themes might you explore?*

» *What benefits might there be for you?*

» *What benefits might there be for your learners and/or your colleagues?*

» *How might it enhance your professional development?*

» *Who might support you?*

CASE STUDY

Kate's action research project

Extract two: reflecting on action and learning

In this extract, Kate is reflecting on some of the things she has learnt from the brainstorming session she had with her learners.

My learners were enthusiastic about the project and so we set aside some time to brainstorm and share our ideas on how we might work together to improve our communication. It was very productive and between us we have a number of ideas we can try out and see what happens. But something came up in the brainstorming session that has left me with egg on my face. My learners have mentioned something that I do that I'd not been aware of. In class discussions I have a habit of not allowing anyone to carry on talking for too long, even on those occasions when what they are saying is pertinent. It seems I jump in and ask someone else if they have anything to contribute, and I prod and cajole those who are less keen to contribute; 'a bit protective' was how they described it.

Initially I was taken aback but now think they may be right – I am overprotective but why? Perhaps I want everyone involved. I know I worry about everyone getting a chance to speak – I don't want anyone getting left out. So I suppose it's about fairness and inclusion but I can see that it can be taken too far. And they are right; they do need to be allowed to get on with their discussions.

Kate continues to reflect and focuses on finding reasons for her actions and sometime later she records some further thoughts and her conclusions on the brainstorming session.

I have had some more thoughts about being overprotective. If I'm honest I believe it's not just about fairness and inclusion. I reckon I probably feel happier keeping control of the discussions. In fact, I'm probably happier keeping control of a lot of what goes on in my classes. It makes me feel comfortable but perhaps it isn't the best thing for my learners.

I have learned some valuable things from just this one session with my learners. Firstly we have some great ideas on improving communication that we can put into practice. Secondly, I have learned that this particular group wants more autonomy in managing their discussions. I don't know yet whether my other groups will feel the same but this is something I can explore.

Thirdly I have learned something about my values. When I was doing the background reading for my action research I read that our values inform our actions but I couldn't really get my head around how this works out in practice. Now I have first-hand experience of it: one of the reasons I intervene in group discussions is because I value fairness and inclusion but the other reason is because I value that feeling of being in control of things. Seeing my values in action has been a potent learning experience.

In the future there will be occasions when intervention is the wise thing to do but my plan is to be more open to what each situation requires and be sensitive to the learners' needs rather than do what's most comfortable for me.

Kate begins her journal extract with a comment about sharing ideas on how she and her learners might work together to improve communication. This is important. It shows that she believes that working together with her learners as equal partners is the best way to achieve her aims. And her belief appears to have been justified. Although we do not know the outcome of the brainstorming session we do know that it produced lots of ideas for trying out. Action research is collaborative and participative, a point noted by McNiff and Whitehead who suggest that action research is:

> *... located in and influenced by a wider environment including human interactions. Action research has to be participatory because the practice we are investigating is always in relation with other people. When we evaluate our practice this refers to the influence of our practice in other people's lives. When we generate new knowledge it is of how we are in relation to others and the theories we produce show the process of how we have developed our practices.*
>
> (McNiff with Whitehead, 2002, p 36)

Reflecting on the brainstorming session with her learners, Kate makes a number of discoveries. The first is that her learners need to be given more autonomy in their discussions. The second is that they may need to be given more responsibility for their own learning. Her third discovery is more personal. Initially Kate believed her actions were informed by her values of fairness and inclusion, but in a reflective process where she continued to question her actions, she identified how much she valued maintaining some degree of control of the learning process. The chances are she felt uncomfortable with this new knowledge yet she used it as a learning opportunity.

One more point can be gleaned from Kate's journal and it is to do with a difference in perspective. Kate believed she was operating a fair and inclusive system. Yet her learners felt she was being over-protective. You might say Kate's learners saw things differently. This state of affairs is not unusual. You probably have your own experiences of learners seeing things differently; different perspectives, assumptions, values, feelings and so on. Kate's learners were confident enough to voice their views in the brainstorming session and Kate was open to what they told her, prepared to search for a full explanation of her actions and then to change her thinking. This openness and change in thinking is important. McNiff and Whitehead suggest that:

> *... action researchers ... try to find ways of accommodating multiple values perspectives. Studying our practice and its underpinning assumptions enables us to develop a creative understanding of ourselves and our own processes of learning and growth. When we do action research we make our thinking different.*
>
> (McNiff and Whitehead, 2002, p 17)

Critical thinking activity

Reflect on your own values. You might find the following questions helpful.

»   *How might they inform your practice?*

»   *Which of them do you see as having a positive influence and how is this evident?*

»   *Can you identify any that might have a negative influence and how is this evident?*

CASE STUDY

Kate's action research project

Extract three: reflecting on action, change and feedback

In this extract Kate is reflecting on what happened when some of the suggestions from the brainstorming session were put into practice, on changes made to her initial aims and on what she has learnt from the feedback she has received from Mira.

One of the comments that came from the brainstorming session was to do with politeness and courtesy. The general feeling was that although they had a sense that politeness and courtesy were pretty much old-fashioned these days, they thought this was a shame and Josie put forward the suggestion that we take just one example of politeness and run with it to see how it feels. So the decision was taken for all of us to think about greetings – not a rigid approach but just to think about each other and how we interact when we arrive and leave.

This suggestion has been in place now for over a fortnight and it has made quite a difference. We evaluated it this morning and the general consensus is that it is making us more aware of each other and more sensitive to each other and we are definitely going to continue with it. We are now planning to trial some of the other suggestions from the brainstorming session. What is interesting is that this raised level of awareness appears to be leading to a whole new area for us to focus on, developing greater co-operation and support within the learner group. This is really good feedback for me as it gives me confidence that we are benefitting from what we are doing.

I originally intended that my action research project would involve just my learners and myself. However, having read about and reflected on the benefits of collaboration, I decided to ask my colleagues whether any of them might be interested in participating and two of them decided to join me. They have both now also involved some of their learners. Mira was very supportive and suggested we extend it to include other colleagues who want to be involved and she would like to be the first one.

There are now six of us and we meet up together over a coffee to see how things are going and to help each other with some suggestions and feedback. We have already begun to make some positive changes in the way we communicate with each other. Apart from Mira we all work part time so sometimes we don't receive important information. At one of our coffee meetings Helen suggested that we set up a communication system that lets others know when we are out of contact and where messages can be left. It's in the early stages at the moment; we are monitoring its success informally, but will do a full evaluation at the end of this coming week when the trial period finishes.

Mira has now given me some feedback on my communication style. Her comments have been pretty positive and she has made some suggestions for further development. She has, however, come up with something I didn't expect. She told me that at team meetings I tend to keep a low profile even though from her experience, whenever I make a contribution it is always pertinent. She asked me if I do this on purpose as she wondered whether I want to make sure everyone else gets a turn to speak – has someone from my business skills group been talking to her? She thinks I could be more proactive, not be concerned about taking responsibility for the others in the team but think about what I want to say. She's right in a way – I don't say too much at meetings, but she's got it so totally wrong about why I do it.

When I know what's going to come up and have had a chance to prepare something there's no problem – it's much the same as preparing for a class. But there's this expectation at meetings that you'll contribute something worthwhile to whatever is being discussed. Even if you know little about it, even if you haven't been forewarned and had a chance to prepare you should be able to come up with some useful ideas. Others in the team seem able to do this easily. They can think on the spot, I can't. It is just not one of my skills. It's not that I don't have things to say, I do, and sometimes more useful things than those suggested by others. I just don't have the confidence to voice them unless I have had time to think, to make sure that what I am saying makes sense. I know it's confidence – I think I see the others as more knowledgeable than I am and I'm frightened of looking stupid. I would like to be more vocal in meetings especially, as I know I've had some good ideas in the past and not voiced them. I just don't know what to do about it.

Kate begins reflecting by recording the monitoring of the *greetings* trial and its success gives her confidence in her choice of topic. She writes about greater awareness within the group leading to a new area on which to focus attention: developing greater co-operation within the learner group. This is a good illustration of the cyclical nature of action research, of Kolb's experiential learning cycle and of Lewin's spiral steps. As you complete one cycle of reflection, planning and action, new ideas and possibilities present themselves. Kate continues by describing how her colleagues have joined in; her initial small-scale ideas have expanded and she is now collaborating with her colleagues as well as her learners. This is an example of the changing nature of action research as it responds to what is happening and to the people around you, a point noted by Valsa Koshy:

> *initial plans quickly become obsolete in the light of learning from experience ... the process is likely to be fluid, open and responsive.*
>
> (Koshy, 2010, p 4)

Kate has recorded another example of something she does, or in this case does not do, which has been observed by someone, in this case Mira her line manager. She misses opportunities to put her views forward at meetings. She feels uncomfortable with this knowledge even though she is aware of its validity. There are two points to consider here. The first is to do with uncertainty. The nature of action research is such that it raises issues but it does not necessarily provide answers and sometimes, as Kate has discovered, it means living with uncertainty: she wants to be more proactive in meetings but does not know what to do about it.

The second point is about emotions. As you saw in an earlier chapter, some emotions can be disruptive. Kate knows that she does not speak out at meetings because she lacks confidence in her ability to think on her feet – she is frightened of looking stupid. Kate's fear is a disruptive emotion; it gets in the way of her professional development and she would rather not feel it. One of the difficulties we have when emotions disrupt is that it is not easy to recognise what is happening. Mira brought something she had observed to Kate's attention, and through reflecting critically on Mira's feedback Kate identified the fear that was informing her actions. Recognising disruptive emotions is the first step in managing them so although Kate does not yet realise it, she is already on the road to solving her problem.

Critical thinking activity

»   *Reflect on your own emotions. Can you identify any that you would say are disruptive? In what way do you think they inform your professional practice?*

CASE STUDY

Kate's action research project

Extract four: reflecting on learning from experience

In this final extract, Kate is reflecting on the experience of engaging in action research, what she has learned from it and how it has changed her thinking.

When I began my action research project I had two things in mind, the first to improve my communication with my learners and second to improve the communication between my learners. Well, that has happened – we are all now much more aware of the importance of good communication and what it entails. But things have changed and the project has changed. It began with one group of my learners and myself, but it has grown to include colleagues and other learners. This has been all to the good; I know my colleagues and my learners better and I have learned from them and I think we have all gained from better understanding of each other. And working together has opened up new practical possibilities not only for me to pursue with my learners but for us as a group of colleagues to continue to develop our communication with each other.

The biggest change has been to do with the focus of my action research, especially the focus of my reflection. I hadn't realised at the start how personal the experience was going to be and how much I was going to learn about myself. I don't just mean about how I interact with learners and colleagues in a practical way, although that has been a big part, but about personal things like my values and my emotions. What I have learned about myself has sometimes been hard to digest, such as being scared of saying something stupid at the team meetings. But through reflecting on what was actually happening and why it was happening, I have learned that I can reduce my anxieties by focusing on the others in the team, thinking more about them and less about myself. This knowledge has increased my confidence so it has been immensely helpful.

The focus of my reflection has changed in another personal way too. Having begun with my professional life firmly under the microscope I now have no doubt that what I have learned through reflecting on my professional practice is just as valid in my personal life. For example, I now see that I do sometimes want to control situations and it shows in my relationships with the various members of my family and even with friends. So this has got me thinking more generally that action research can have benefits for me not only in a professional capacity but as an individual. I suppose I now think of reflection and action research as being relevant to my life as a whole.

When I began this project I remember writing in my journal that I valued the freedom of being able to decide what I wanted to research and how I wanted to do it. And that still stands but I now feel that the critical reflection I have been doing as part of my action research itself is even more freeing. When researching action research I sometimes came across critical reflection described as empowering or emancipatory and at the time I didn't really catch on what they were getting at but I do now – it gives me the tools to better manage my life both professionally and personally and that feeling is liberating.

Critical thinking activity

» *What is your opinion of Kate's decision to make action research a part of her personal as well as her professional life? Evaluate the benefits that Kate mentions. Identify any disadvantages.*

When you set out to do action research you are likely to have a good idea of what you want to achieve and even if your research is more about trying out ideas, experimenting to see what happens, you will at least have some sense of the direction you want to go in. Yet action research often does not fit conveniently into preconceived ideas and plans. It develops and changes through the experience of participating in it as new ideas and themes emerge. Kate envisaged a *small-scale specific* action research project. Yet it developed into something larger and broader in scope as colleagues and other learners participated in it. You may also be focusing on a practical issue but then find as Kate did that some of the discoveries you make are personal, informed by your values or influenced by your emotions.

The experience of engaging in action research provided Kate with a range of new knowledge. Some of this knowledge was theoretical, for example, she learnt from the background reading around her topic. Some of it was practical: improved communication skills come into this category. Yet by far her greatest learning came from experience, from engaging in the experience of action research itself, from the interactions with learners and colleagues and from the feedback she received from them which enabled her to reflect and learn.

Knowledge gained from experience

It is worthwhile to include here some general comments concerning knowledge. As you saw from the above case study, knowledge comes in a number of guises. It can be theoretical, information that you might learn from background reading around a topic. It can be practical, as in the knowledge you gain, for example, when developing communication skills. It can also be knowledge that you learn from your experience, from interacting, negotiating and collaborating with others. You will likely identify a connection between these three forms of knowledge – theoretical, practical and experiential mentioned here – and the concept of espoused theory and theory in use discussed in earlier chapters.

The knowledge that is gained from experience is sometimes viewed as having less value than theoretical or practical knowledge; it is sometimes seen as perhaps less robust, or as personal, subjective and intuitive. Mary Midgley provides a different perspective, highlighting the complexity of knowledge itself and the value and legitimacy of personal experience.

> We exist ... as interdependent parts of a complex network ... as for our knowledge it too is a network involving all kinds of lateral links, a system in which the most varied kinds of connection may be relevant for helping us to meet various kinds of question. ... Much of the time we use whatever forms of thought turn out to be needed. ... Often it is our powers of perception that are central to the work rather than consecutive reasoning that can easily be tested. And in any human situation we must call on special powers of social perception and imagination that are not really formulable at all.
>
> (Midgley, 2007, pp 25, 26)

Midgley's comments are a pertinent reminder that when you undertake action research you create your own knowledge. It may relate to a specific context but this does not make it of any less value. You learn from your experience of engaging with it and others can refer to your research and learn from it in exactly the same way as they would from any other piece of research.

There is one final point to be taken from Kate's journal entries: the knowledge she gained from experience enabled her to regard both action research and reflection as having a place in her personal as well as her professional life. It makes sense of course to take this more holistic approach; if reflecting can support you in developing your professional life why discard it at the end of the working day? This was a natural progression for Kate, as it was clear from her very first journal extract that reflection was already a regular part of her professional life. Reflection gave her self-knowledge; this self-knowledge gave her greater control over both her professional and her personal life and she discovered that the experience was empowering.

There is no shortage of writers who recognise this empowering aspect. Cooper (Moon, 2010), for example, referring to reflective journals sees them as:

... a way to tell our own story, a way to learn who we have been, who we are and who we are becoming. We literally become teachers and researchers in our own lives, empowering ourselves in the process.

(Cooper, 1991, cited Moon, 2010, p 192)

Paul McIntosh puts it slightly differently. In writing about action research he suggests that it:

... in broad terms concerns the lived experience of people and the understanding of the essences of reality. It therefore has two main thrusts: knowledge ... and empowerment through the process of people constructing and using their own knowledge.

(McIntosh, 2010, p 53)

In summary, the knowledge you create from the experience of engaging in an action research project is not only valid but is professionally and personally empowering.

Conclusion

You will find a wide selection of practical books to help you in doing action research; two are mentioned at the end of this chapter. Yet practical guides along with action research models are there in a supportive role. Your action research should remain just that: yours.

This chapter has highlighted the central role of reflection in action research and has hopefully inspired you to engage in your own action research as a means not only to enhance your professional life but also to enrich your personal life. In an earlier chapter you were asked to '*imagine yourself as a project that you are going to research; an exploration of what you do and why you do it*'. Nowhere is this mindset more helpful than in doing action research. If you are inspired, you will be joining a long tradition of thinkers and philosophers going back more than two millennia who understood and welcomed self-knowledge as a route to wisdom.

Chapter reflections

» *Action research incorporates a number of theories and approaches but exhibits core features: critical reflection, action, collaboration and emancipation. Critical reflection lies at the heart of action research.*

» *When you undertake action research you create your own knowledge from the experience, knowledge that has as much validity as theoretical and/or practical knowledge.*

» *Reflection in action research is ongoing. It requires you to consider your values and your emotions and how they inform your actions. Uncertainty may be part of the experience.*

» *Action research is just as valid in your personal life as in your professional life. Models and research guides can provide a framework to support you but your action research is owned and controlled by you. This autonomy is empowering.*

Taking it further

Koshy, V (2010) *Action Research for Improving Educational Practice.* London: Sage.

This is a step-by-step guide on what action research is and how to carry it out, presented in a straightforward style and with plenty of examples and case studies.

McNiff, J and Whitehead, J (2010) *You and Your Action Research Project.* Abingdon: Routledge.

The practice of action research and its underlying values are explained here. It includes case studies and describes the various stages of doing an action research project.

Wallace, S (2013) *Doing Research in Further Education and Training.* Exeter: Learning Matters.

Written specifically for teachers and trainers in the FE sector, this accessible guide offers a range of approaches into all aspects of research including action research.

References

Bassey, M (1998) Action Research for Improving Practice, in Halsall, R (ed) *Teacher Research and School Improvement: Opening Doors from the Inside.* Buckingham: OU Press.

Boud, D (2010) Relocating reflection in the context of practice, in Bradbury, H, Frost, N, Carr, W and Kemmis, S (eds) (1986) *Becoming Critical: Education Knowledge and Action Research.* Abingdon: Routledge.

Carr, W and Kemmis, S (1986) *Becoming Critical: Education, Knowledge and Action Research.* London: The Falmer Press.

Elliott, J (1991) *Action Research for Educational Change.* Buckingham: OU Press.

Kilminster, S and Zukas, M (eds) *Beyond Reflective Practice: New Approaches to Professional Lifelong Learning.* Abingdon: Routledge.

Koshy, V (2010) *Action Research for Improving Educational Practice.* London: Sage.

Lewin, K (1946) Action Research and Minority Problems. *Journal of Social Issues,* 2(4): 34–46.

McIntosh, P (2010) *Action Research and Reflective Practice: Creative and Visual Methods to Facilitate Reflection and Learning.* London: Routledge.

McNiff, J with Whitehead, J (2002) *Action Research: Principles and Practice.* London: Routledge.

Midgley, M (2007) *The Myths We Live By.* London: Routledge.

Moon, J (2010) *Reflection in Learning & Professional Development.* Abingdon: Routledge Falmer.

Stenhouse, L (1975) *An Introduction to Curriculum Research and Development.* London: Heinemann.

Zeni, J (1998) A Guide to Ethical Issues and Action Research. *Educational Action Research,* 6(1): 9–19.

Websites

www.open.ac.uk/cobe/docs/AR-Guide-final.pdf (accessed February 2015)

10 Conclusion

Some people change the world. One such was Charles Darwin, whose theory of the origin of species and the idea that natural selection was the driving force of evolutionary development revolutionised the way in which we now see the world and our place in it. You would be hard pressed to find a better example of a reflective practitioner than Charles Darwin. All the features of good reflective practice are evident from the way in which he worked.

He was a meticulous observer of geological features, flora and fauna over an extended period of time. He kept extraordinarily detailed notes of his observations and theoretical speculations, developing his ideas and recording his reflections in an ever-expanding series of notebooks. This vast library of notebooks, compiled over a quarter of a century, bears witness to his meticulous recording of his observations and developing ideas. His sources were wide-ranging: a diverse range of reading, collaboration with experts and discussions with specialists from many different areas of expertise.

Darwin was always aware of the danger of presenting a one-sided view; he was never completely satisfied with his ideas and was constantly searching for new perspectives to ensure that he presented an inclusive and balanced picture. In addition, he was intensely curious, full of wonder at the natural world, optimistic, creative and open to a variety of possibilities. He combined this with a rigorous objectivity based on scientific observation. He constantly tested and revised his conclusions in the light of new evidence and interpretations. In short, he was a reflective practitioner *par excellence*.

You could also view Darwin's adult life as one enormous action research project. It is certainly not difficult to identify the action research features of reflection, action, collaboration and empowerment in his endeavours to explain the origin of species. He was constantly reflecting on his observations and discoveries and questioning his findings, searching for explanations and testing new theories. He involved many others in his research, such as Richard Owen who studied the fossils that Darwin had collected during his travels and John Gould who identified the many species of finch that Darwin had found on the Galapagos

Islands. Finally, Darwin's rigorous scientific and objective methods empowered him to continue his investigations against a background of often virulent opposition. There is no doubt that his work opened the way to new learning and knowledge.

FE teachers also change the world, albeit on a smaller scale than Charles Darwin. You change your learners' lives: open metaphorical doors for them, encourage them to discover more about themselves and the world around them, help them to fulfil their potential. In doing so, you not only develop your teaching skills but also gain a unique satisfaction that comes from helping others. It is a rewarding job, even though there are the inevitable frustrations to overcome: lack of time, filling in complicated forms, working within organisations that are constantly struggling with bureaucratic intervention and insufficient resources. Here is a final story to illustrate this point. It concerns Alan, an experienced teacher who used to love his work but who is now finding life in an FE college increasingly difficult.

CASE STUDY

Alan's story: who is the real mentor?

I can't believe I'm writing this, given how I felt a year ago when I was asked to be a mentor to Charlotte, one of my staff who is undertaking a PGCE course. It was yet another job on top of the load of tasks I was trying to cram in every day before going home exhausted and having a pile of marking and half a dozen reports to write! But I knew Charlotte could become a really good teacher and she clearly wanted me to help her so I agreed to do the job.

I began to wonder what I'd let myself in for when I read what I had to do. I would have to not only observe her teaching and have regular tutorials but also read and comment on her reflective journal. I had this vision of having to plough through pages and pages of detail about what went on in her lessons and trying to think of something useful to say to her. Yet more death by paperwork!

Now, it is one year later. Charlotte has her PGCE and I reckon I've learned more from Charlotte than she has from me. What I've seen has been the change of an enthusiastic but somewhat disorganised and under-confident teacher into someone who is perceptive, organised and highly professional. And the key reason for this change has been that journal that I was so dismissive about at the start of her course. The thing is that Charlotte is a natural writer who is good at putting her feelings down on paper, being honest about her problems and determined about getting better at her job. She often used words and phrases like 'exciting', 'rewarding', 'making a difference'. Right from the start we were able to discuss the issues that she wrote about and work through possible solutions that she could try out and then we'd discuss it some more. And when it worked, she was so keen to tell me what happened that it reminded me of the enthusiasm I used to have but which has become a bit dormant.

Consequently, the realisation gradually dawned that Charlotte's problems were mine as well. I still have trouble with difficult classes, I still let my irritations affect how I get on with some learners, I still don't give enough time to think about the good and bad things that happen in my classes and so on. I reflect on my teaching but Charlotte's experience showed me that I could do this a lot better.

The truth is, I'd become lazy and I've used the excuse of pressure of work to avoid dealing with it. Maybe I don't need to write a formal journal, but at least I should give myself a routine where I set aside a regular time each day or week to think about what has happened at work, and capture the conclusions by jotting the main points down somewhere. So this is my resolution for next semester – don't just think and grumble about issues, but find time to reflect critically and positively and share with others. In other words, be like the teacher Charlotte has become.

Nobody would claim that finding time to reflect critically, objectively and systematically will remove all the problems you face on a daily basis as an FE teacher today. The pressures are unrelenting and exhausting. We would claim, however, that, like Alan, allocating time and effort to improve your skills as an effective reflective practitioner is a pretty good way of dealing with these pressures, making your professional life more rewarding and helping you fulfil your own potential.

Appendix 1: Critical incident pro forma

Describe the incident	
Plan what changes to make next time	
Describe what happened when you implemented the changes	
Evaluate how well the changes worked	

Appendix 2: Journal entry sheet

Description – What happened? This might be a course you went on, something you read, a conversation with a colleague, an incident while teaching etc. Think about why you are writing about this particular incident.	
Feelings – What were your thoughts and feelings? Were you excited, cross, motivated, angry, elated etc? What were your thoughts about the situation or occurrence?	
Evaluation – What was good or bad about the experience? Reflect on the positives and negatives. What worked well that you could build on? What needs improving/developing? Why?	
Analysis – What sense can you make of the situation? What did you learn about yourself, your subject, your teaching or your students? Can you make any connections with theory?	
Conclusion – What else could you have done? Consider alternatives and *think outside the box*. Consider whether you would benefit from professional development either in teaching or your subject area. Consider reading/ research and talking to colleagues for ideas.	
Action Plan – What are you going to do? Apply what you have learnt to the described situation or a new similar situation. How is your teaching and learning going to change/develop based on your reflections?	

With thanks to the ITT staff and learners at Grantham College, Lincolnshire.

Appendix 3: ETF Professional Standards for Teachers and Trainers in Education and Training (England)

Introduction

Teachers and trainers are reflective and enquiring practitioners who think critically about their own educational assumptions, values and practice in the context of a changing contemporary and educational world. They draw on relevant research as part of evidence-based practice.

They act with honesty and integrity to maintain high standards of ethics and professional behaviour in support of learners and their expectations.

Teachers and trainers are *dual professionals*; they are both subject and/or vocational specialists and experts in teaching and learning. They are committed to maintaining and developing their expertise in both aspects of their role to ensure the best outcomes for their learners.

These expectations of teachers and trainers underpin the 2014 professional standards, with their overall purpose being to support teachers and trainers to maintain and improve knowledge and standards of teaching and learning, and outcomes for learners.

The professional standards are set across three sections each of equal importance: each links to and supports the other sections.

The 2014 professional standards:

1. set out clear expectations of effective practice in Education and Training;

2. enable teachers and trainers to identify areas for their own professional development;

3. support initial teacher education;

4. provide a national reference point that organisations can use to support the development of their staff.

Professional standards

As a professional teacher or trainer, you should demonstrate commitment to the following in your professional practice.

Professional values and attributes

Develop your own judgement of what works and does not work in your teaching and training.

1. Reflect on what works best in your teaching and learning to meet the diverse needs of learners.

2. Evaluate and challenge your practice, values and beliefs.

3. Inspire, motivate and raise aspirations of learners through your enthusiasm and knowledge.

4. Be creative and innovative in selecting and adapting strategies to help learners to learn.

5. Value and promote social and cultural diversity, equality of opportunity and inclusion.

6. Build positive and collaborative relationships with colleagues and learners.

Professional knowledge and understanding

Develop deep and critically informed knowledge and understanding in theory and practice.

7. Maintain and update knowledge of your subject and/or vocational area.

8. Maintain and update your knowledge of educational research to develop evidence-based practice.

9. Apply theoretical understanding of effective practice in teaching, learning and assessment, drawing on research and other evidence.

10. Evaluate your practice with others and assess its impact on learning.

11. Manage and promote positive learner behaviour.

12. Understand the teaching and professional role and your responsibilities.

Professional skills

Develop your expertise and skills to ensure the best outcomes for learners.

13. Motivate and inspire learners to promote achievement and develop their skills to enable progression.

14. Plan and deliver effective learning programmes for diverse groups or individuals in a safe and inclusive environment.

15. Promote the benefits of technology and support learners in its use.

16. Address the mathematics and English needs of learners and work creatively to overcome individual barriers to learning.

17. Enable learners to share responsibility for their own learning and assessment, setting goals that stretch and challenge.

18. Apply appropriate and fair methods of assessment and provide constructive and timely feedback to support progression and achievement.

19. Maintain and update your teaching and training expertise and vocational skills through collaboration with employers.

20. Contribute to organisational development and quality improvement through collaboration with others.

Index